ADDICTIONARY

/ə-'dik-shən er-ē\

n. pl-naries [C addict, addiction, dictionary] (2009)

1: a reference book containing examples along with information about different kinds of addictions. **2:** a reference book listing terms or names important to a particular addiction along with their meanings and applications. **3:** a book of self-tests one can take to determine whether one might be addicted to someone or something.

TIM CHAPMAN, MSC.D., CSAC

Emerald Books

an imprint of Fideli Publishing, Inc.

ADDICTIONARY

A dictionary of over 75 addictions

Illustrations Descriptions Tests

Illustrations: Marita A. Alaniz

Edited: James Warder

©Copyright 2009, Tim Chapman, Msc.D., CSAC

Revised 2003
Original printing 1993

ISBN: 978-1-60414-156-6

Introduction

I am an Alcoholic. My primary addiction is to alcohol. All of my other addictions are secondary and are symptoms of my primary addiction. These secondary addictions may include relationships, chocolate and work, just to name a few. However, they are dangerous in that they have great potential to lead me back to my lethal drug of choice, alcohol. Others I meet may have a primary addiction to food, sex or what have you. In their cases, alcohol may lead them back into their primary addiction. Primary addictions are life threatening if left untreated.

For the past twenty-five years of my life I have worked as a professional counselor treating addictions. What I have discovered is that virtually anything that is mood-or mind-altering can become an addiction. Furthermore, most people have dual addictions. My belief is that everyone has an addiction in one form or another.

My intent in writing this book is not to fix anyone's addiction, but to educate them about addiction. This may help to eliminate the stigma attached to it. My hope is that this will enable people to "come out of the closet" and receive the help they need in order to address their primary addiction while recognizing how all secondary-addictions contribute to the first. In order to keep one's primary addictions in remission, one must also address any secondary addiction(s).

Codependency is an addiction in and of itself, yet it seems appropriate for me to say that all secondary addictions could be called codependent traits or Codependent illness depending upon its severity.

I do not intend for this book to be a diagnostic tool. It is based on interviews I have conducted over the past 25 years with people afflicted with addictions. Although addiction is a serious problem, I have written this book with some humor in hopes of helping the reader to ease the digestion of the subject matter.

Once people recognize their addictions, I recommend they seek professional help immediately. Addiction counselors are their best source of information for assistance. When seeking a doctor to help with an addiction problem, one should ask about the doctor's previous experience in treating addictions, including the outcome. If a person is not comfortable with a clinician's answer, he/she should seek assistance elsewhere.

The reader will notice in this book that all addictions possess the same Major Symptoms, as well as similar characteristics, regardless of the addiction. I have not included all the symptoms of a particular addiction for professional diagnosis; however, these symptoms are real and do indicate a problem which usually requires professional help.

Twelve Step groups, such as Alcoholics Anonymous, Codependents Anonymous or Overeaters Anonymous, are very helpful in the recovery from addictions. I recommend that addicts attend the group(s) that best meet their needs. They should not however, attend 12-step programs in place of professional therapy.

In this book I do not pass judgment on the addictions listed. Rather, I illuminate the addictive process that people may engage in surrounding the addiction. Take for instance an addiction to shopping. Shopping in and of it self is not judged as good, bad, right or wrong. It is the pre-occupation with shopping or the loss of control in one's life, which leads to excessive shopping that is the key to the addiction.

I have gathered the Major Symptoms listed in this book from several sources, including from men, women, boys and girls who have suffered from some sort of addiction.

I hope you are both entertained and enlightened by this book.

Table of Contents

PART ONE

Characteristics of Addiction

There are normally four (4) characteristics of addiction. Addiction is not a temporary state. It is an ongoing chronic process and, in many cases, can be fatal if untreated. The four characteristics are:

PRIMARY
PROGRESSIVE
CHRONIC
FATAL

1. **PRIMARY**
   The addiction is not a symptom of another problem. It is the PRIMARY problem in addicts' lives. It must be handled FIRST. Furthermore, if this process is not interrupted first, no other significant progress can be made. For instance, an alcoholic with a relationship problem must first stop drinking and deal with the alcoholism before the relationship issue can be addressed.

2. **PROGRESSIVE**

   The process of addiction gets worse as time goes on (as described in the · Process of Addiction · section in this book).

3. **CHRONIC**

   The addiction is always present, constantly weakening and troubling the person.

4. **FATAL**
   The addiction has life damaging consequences and, in time, causes premature death.

PART TWO

Process of Addiction

There are four (4) stages involved in the process of addiction:

1. LEARNING THE ADDICTIVE PROCESS
2. SEEKING THE ADDICTIVE PROCESS
3. PSYCHOLOGICAL ADDICTION
4. PHYSICAL ADDICTION/CONSEQUENCE

1. LEARNING THE ADDICTIVE PROCESS

Anything new (positive or negative) begins in the learning stage. Addicts engage innocently and experimentally in the process. In the learning stage of an addictive process, they experience a "reward." The reward is a mood swing or an altered physical and/or emotional sensation that is usually euphoric. In the learning stage, they normally experience three (3) aspects of the mood swing:

LEARNING THE MOOD SWING
TESTING THE MOOD SWING
TRUSTING THE MOOD SWING
LEARNING THE MOOD SWING:

Here, they engage in the process and learn what it does to their mood. If they have a positive experience in the mood swing, they will continue on to the next phase. If not, they will discontinue the process at this point, thus eliminating any further activity that may possibly lead to addiction.

TESTING THE MOOD SWING:

Here, addicts continue into the process by experimenting (consciously or unconsciously). They will determine how much of a mood swing is adequate, acceptable or tolerable. At this point, they may determine to discontinue the process thus avoiding the possibility of addiction. If they continue to favor the mood altering reward at this point, they then move into the next aspect of the "Learning the Mood Swing" stage that has addictive qualities about it - "Trusting the Mood Swing."

TRUSTING THE MOOD SWING:

Here, they have reached a phase that could be the potentially addictive element. They have trusted a mood-altering process. This in and of it-self is not necessarily destructive. However, in this phase the victims may potentially need to repeat a particular process in order to reach the "external reward."

2. SEEKING THE ADDICTIVE PROCESS

In this phase addicts begin looking forward to the mood swing. Here they set boundaries, limits or rules regarding the process. This is the "make it or break it" phase where they either stick to the self-induced rule or lose the ability to uphold the set limits. If the rules are broken, bent or manipulated on a consistent basis (approximately 2-4 times per week for a minimum of 6 months), they have fallen into the next phase of Psychological Addiction.

3. PSYCHOLOGICAL ADDICTION

In this stage addicts have an emotional, psychological, social or cognitive need to continue to repeat the process. They experience consequences as results of the process yet continue the process. This is the stage in which the Major Symptoms will appear. In this phase the consequences are usually emotional pain (e.g., embarrassment over behavior exhibited as a direct or indirect result of the destructive process) or causing pain or harm to others. Despite these consequences and after sincere efforts to control, cut back on or stop the process, these people still have a need to repeat it. This process happens much quicker in children; the life-damaging effects happen in a few months to a few years. In adults the process may take years to recognize by an untrained person.

4. **PHYSICAL ADDICTION/CONSEQUENCE**

The final stage of all addictions is Physical Addiction. Most people think of addicts as those who have reached physical and spiritual bankruptcy and that they cannot possibly be addicted without physical evidence of the problem. Hogwash!! We need to be aware that once they reach this stage of development in the addictive process, it is extremely difficult to reverse the effects. In this book, physical or "late stage" symptoms will be discussed as they apply to a particular addiction. It is extremely important to know the early warning signs of an addictive process in order to be able to facilitate an intervention and ensure that these people avoid the chronic and fatal stage of addiction. It is also important to know that fatality is common in the psychological stage of addiction. Physical consequences may be manifested directly or indirectly in an addictive process.

PART THREE

Major Symptoms of Addiction

There are four (4) Major Symptoms that accompany all addictions which are almost always present. In order to make an accurate diagnosis, one should be able to see Major Symptoms being exhibited by the addict. These symptoms will accompany other unique characteristics of a particular addiction. The four major symptoms are:

1. LOSS OF CONTROL
2. PREOCCUPATION
3. TOLERANCE
4. DENIAL

1. LOSS OF CONTROL

This symptom is an inability to abstain from a destructive process despite personal attempts to stop by using sheer willpower. This may include, but is not limited to:

- making promises to stop and not following through;

- repeating the same destructive behavior over and over despite the consequences.

2. PREOCCUPATION

When people exhibit this symptom, their thoughts, conversations or actions revolve around a particular addictive process. This may include, but is not limited to:

- constantly thinking about the process;
- defending the destructive process;
- planning their lives around the process;
- lying about the process
(even when it is easier to tell the truth).

3. TOLERANCE

People exhibiting this symptom have an increased need to participate in the destructive process. This may include, but is not limited to:

- increasing amounts of the destructive process to reach the desired effect;

- willingness or ability to put up with the increased consequences of the destructive process.

4. DENIAL

Exhibiting this symptom, people will rationalize, minimize, justify or simply not acknowledge the painful truth of the destructive process. This includes, but is not limited to:

- believing "it's not that bad", even when severe consequences are present;

- "sincere delusion or repression" (pain that is excluded from consciousness and left to operate in the unconscious).

PART FOUR

Addiction Scale

The Addiction Scale helps determine one's level of involvement in the addictive process. This book contains tests that people may take for each addiction listed. There are 12 symptoms for each test. Each symptom is significant in its impact on a person's life. The more symptoms one checks, the more severe the problem.

SCALE = 1(mild) -12 (severe)

Number of symptoms:

☐ 1 - Pay attention!

☐ 2 - Pay close attention!!

☐ 3 - BEWARE!!! (Have a serious talk with a trusted friend).

☐ 4 - There is an emotional need to continue the process.

☐ 5 - There is a psychological need to continue the process.

☐ 6 - This is likely an addiction. (Attend a 12-step meeting, such as A.A., O.A., etc).

☐ 7 - Seek a professional evaluation with an addiction counselor, psychologist, etc.

☐ 8 - Well into addiction. Self-esteem is likely to be damaged by now.

☐ 9 - This addiction is chronic; seek counseling and/or treatment.

☐ 10 - Possible loss of "self" at this stage. Seek treatment immediately.

☐ 11 - Physical symptoms are likely present (withdrawal, illness, insomnia, etc.).

☐ 12 - Vicious circle - addiction continues until insanity, death or recovery.

If six or more of these symptoms apply to you or someone else, contact Chapman House listed on the back cover.

PART FIVE

Dictionary
Of
Addictions

ABUSE ADDICTION (PHYSICAL)

"Codependent" is a term used to describe a person who accepts abuse from another and remains in the abusive situation. Abuse Addicts will not only stay in a potentially physically life-threatening situation or relationship, but they might actually instigate the problem by antagonizing the perpetrator. This is considered a chronic case of Codependency. Those who have advanced to this stage have truly lost control of their life. They seem to have a need to be physically harmed by others.

Comment: It may be difficult for some to believe that people can get to this place and not realize it. Not realizing how one got here is a hallmark symptom of the addictive process.

Are you or someone you know addicted to PHYSICAL ABUSE?

Those who are may:

- ☐ Start fights with others knowing physical danger is present.
- ☐ Feel a sense of control after being physically abused.
- ☐ Stay out of relationships with "wimps" or "weaklings".
- ☐ Enjoy the attention received from being abused.
- ☐ Believe the beatings are sometimes deserved.
- ☐ No longer be bothered by being abused, at least not as much as before.
- ☐ Usually keep the abuse a secret (not tell others).
- ☐ Feel a sense of relief after being abused and repeat the pattern.
- ☐ Be abused once a month or more.
- ☐ Have had others express concern over the abusive situation.
- ☐ Consider getting help but never do so.
- ☐ Require medical attention at times due to abuse.

(Check page 9 for the Addiction Scale)

ACTIVITY ADDICTION

Those who suffer from this addiction are always doing something and never relaxing. They have racing thoughts to the point of exhaustion. This may be an effort to avoid unpleasant feelings. Keeping busy to keep busy is the idea here. The real danger is that society validates this type of behavior by labeling these people as hard workers or productive, never seeing that they may be in tremendous emotional trouble.

Are you or someone you know addicted to ACTIVITY?

Those who are may:

☐ Rarely, if ever, take time for themselves.

☐ Be overly involved in others' affairs.

☐ Belong to several clubs while resenting it.

☐ Always volunteer to do things for others.

☐ Have difficulty relaxing.

☐ Regularly over schedule themselves.

☐ Usually be in a hurry.

☐ Rarely finish projects they start.

☐ Have difficulty saying no to others' requests.

☐ Have racing thoughts much of the time.

☐ Feel exhausted much of the time.

☐ Rarely feel finished with things.

(Check page 9 for the Addiction Scale)

ALCOHOL ADDICTION

As with many addictions, Alcohol Addiction is a disease. Without intervention and treatment, it will progressively get worse and end in premature death. Alcoholics will exhibit irrational behavior as a result of the use of alcohol. Those closest to them will also experience loss of control in their lives. It is up to those who first recognize this problem in another to seek professional help for themselves and the addicted person. It is very common to deny the problem or not believe it is a problem. Most people think alcoholics must be physically ill from drinking or be skid row bums. Nonsense! The disease begins long before physical problems arise. When psychological symptoms are recognized, that is the time for intervention.

Are you or someone you know addicted to ALCOHOL?

Those who are may:

☐ Experience loss of, or possible loss of a job/education due to drinking.

☐ Drink to build self-confidence.

☐ Drink alone.

☐ Find that drinking affects their reputation.

☐ Find that their drinking is painful to others.

☐ Feel guilty about drinking.

☐ Crave alcohol at a certain time of day.

☐ Experience legal problems because of drinking.

☐ Attempt to quit drinking without success.

☐ Think about drinking much of the time.

☐ Experience memory loss due to drinking (blackouts).

☐ Have thoughts like "I may have a problem with alcohol."

(Check page 9 for the Addiction Scale)

ANGER ADDICTION

Anger Addicts are often in a vicious circle with anger. They are difficult for others to be close to. Others sense fear and distance from them and may also feel intimidated and unwelcome in their lives. Anger, many times, is the feeling that covers other undesirable feelings, such as hurt, sadness, fear, shame, etc. Those addicted to anger usually dislike the behavior associated with it as much as others do. They feel out of control and unable to stop the angry outbursts. This is very destructive to intimate relationships. These people react to most undesirable news with anger. They don't usually stop to see if there may be other feelings. They usually regret the anger outbursts. As with most addictions, it usually takes someone other than the addict to see the problem and reach out for help.

Are you or someone you know addicted to ANGER?

Those who are may:

☐ Feel relief only after expressing intense anger.

☐ Keep anger secret until they blow up.

☐ Feel guilty for having anger.

☐ Attempt to control angry outbursts without success.

☐ Have an intense need to express anger to get what they want (control the situation).

☐ Constantly blame others for their anger.

☐ Rarely express anger appropriately or directly.

☐ Plan arguments or fights with others.

☐ Intimidate others with anger.

☐ Find that their own anger scares or concerns them and/or others.

☐ Suffer physical problems as a result of anger/depression.

☐ Find that others are concerned about their anger.

(Check page 9 for the Addiction Scale)

ARGUING ADDICTION

Arguing Addicts have a tremendous need to argue with others. This may be an effort to project undesirable feelings onto others to avoid the pain. These people will argue even when they know they are wrong. It is as though they have nothing better to do than to argue with others. They usually live a lonely existence due to extreme fear of being wrong or of being found out by others. As ironic as it may seem, sometimes arguing is the only way these people can feel bonded or close to another person. Feeling a deeper sense of loneliness after an argument creates more anxiety and a greater need to argue. This is the vicious cycle of Arguing Addiction.

Are you or someone you know addicted to ARGUING?

Those who are may:

☐ Feel at a loss for words unless arguing.

☐ Often be hurtful to others by arguing.

☐ Lose friends because of constant arguing.

☐ Have a need to be right nearly all the time.

☐ Be rigid and not seem to listen to others.

☐ Intentionally plan arguments with others.

☐ Lose a job or be expelled from school due to arguing.

☐ Find that others complain or are fed up with the arguing.

☐ Feel fear much of the time and need to defend someone or something.

☐ Find that their arguing has become more severe and more frequent.

☐ Feel remorseful after arguing yet continue anyway.

☐ Argue with authority figures without considering the consequences.

(Check page 9 for the Addiction Scale)

ATTENTION ADDICTION

Attention Addicts have an insatiable need for attention. There never seems to be enough time in the spotlight for them. Others may resent these "attention hogs" yet are uncomfortable confronting them. These people are rarely in touch with personal feelings. They may have suffered "emotional malnutrition" as children and now find addictive needs to fulfill that are rarely, if ever satisfied. They are usually feeling inadequate and desperate for love and cannot understand why others are distant or non-appreciative of their efforts. This insatiable need may lead to physical illness due to stress.

Are you or someone you know addicted to ATTENTION?

Those who are may:

- [ ] Usually need to be the center of attention at a party.
- [ ] Always feel left out when not chosen to participate.
- [ ] Do bizarre or inappropriate things for attention (age inappropriate).
- [ ] Feel more worthless than others.
- [ ] Regularly manipulate others to get attention.
- [ ] Get into trouble trying to get attention/approval.
- [ ] Embarrass others with attention-seeking behavior.
- [ ] Have lost friendships due to attention-seeking behavior.
- [ ] Be willing to give up money to get attention.
- [ ] Usually feel depressed when alone.
- [ ] Find that others are concerned about their need for attention.
- [ ] Fear their needs will never be met.

(Check page 9 for the Addiction Scale)

BLAMING ADDICTION

Many people become addicted to blaming in an effort to avoid responsibility for their actions and the associated consequences. One theory is that they may have been blamed for all the problems in the family while growing up, thus experiencing responsibility as overwhelmingly painful. In this case, however, these people were burdened with ALL responsibility rather than personal responsibility. One can see in this case why these people would attempt to avoid responsibility at all cost. On the other hand, these people may never have been given responsibility or held accountable for their actions as children. In this case, they would search for scapegoats or others to be responsible for them.

Are you or someone you know addicted to BLAMING?

Those who are may:

☐ Constantly manipulate to avoid responsibility.

☐ Frequently gossip about others.

☐ Have a particular person to blame (child, spouse, etc.).

☐ Be quick to point out the faults/shortcomings of others.

☐ Create circumstances to blame others.

☐ Be extremely sensitive when held accountable for a problem.

☐ Blame others for most personal problems.

☐ Lie (even about loved ones) to avoid responsibility.

☐ Find that others feel hopeless about them ever taking responsibility.

☐ Often be depressed or full of self-pity about most things.

☐ Feel desperate when held accountable.

☐ Use anger or violence to intimidate others and avoid responsibility.

(Check page 9 for the Addiction Scale)

CAFFEINE ADDICTION

Caffeine is a mood-altering chemical found in many products, such as coffee, cola, chocolate candy and many other foods. Caffeine is the addictive agent in these products. People become addicted to the mood-altering effect produced by the caffeine. Those addicted to it may go through withdrawal symptoms when stopping the use of the substance abruptly. Craving the chemical is common and noticeable at certain times of the day. A typical statement one might hear is, "Don't talk to that person until he's had his coffee; he is miserable without his first cup of coffee in the morning." That first cup of coffee is a critical symptom of Caffeine Addiction. These people may be using caffeine to feel good (mild euphoria). Those who are addicted to caffeine may continue to use it to avoid feeling bad (withdrawal symptoms). This process is usually not noticeable to most people, including the addicted person.

Are you or someone you know addicted to CAFFEINE?

Those who are may:

☐ Feel angry or irritable when denied the use of caffeine.

☐ Crave caffeine at a certain time of day.

☐ Usually or always have caffeine nearby or available.

☐ Become ill from caffeine yet dismiss the symptoms.

☐ Need to use larger quantities of caffeine since first using it.

☐ Often rely on caffeine to stay awake.

☐ Use caffeine frequently throughout the day.

☐ Feel depressed or exhausted without the use of caffeine.

☐ Regularly hear others joking or talking about their caffeine intake.

☐ Often feel "hyper" or "high" on caffeine.

☐ Attempt to cut down on or stop using caffeine with little success.

☐ Think or suspect there is a problem with caffeine.

(Check page 9 for the Addiction Scale)

CHAOS ADDICTION

Chaos Addicts may be acting out the family situation they grew up in. If they were reared in homes of constant chaos, it becomes safe or familiar to be in constant chaos as adults. They may have an unconscious need to reenact the family scene (chaotic events experienced in childhood) over and over again. In this addiction, they may find peace and serenity very anxiety producing. With uncomfortable peace, they begin to create "family-iliar" (familiar, chaotic scenes in the family while growing up) chaos.

Are you or someone you know addicted to CHAOS?

Those who are may:

- ☐ Often feel a need to create conflict.
- ☐ Constantly be involved with or solving emotional problems.
- ☐ Thrive on chaos/conflict at home or work.
- ☐ Be bored when not dealing with conflict.
- ☐ Become depressed or anxious when things are calm.
- ☐ Have many friends who have major emotional problems.
- ☐ Often be in trouble at work or school.
- ☐ Have more than two sexually intimate relationships at a time.
- ☐ Have a career goal or profession that is crisis oriented (police, fire, etc.).
- ☐ Feel out of control 50% of the time.
- ☐ Be avoided by others attempting to avoid chaos.
- ☐ Feel frustrated from constant chaos yet compelled to do it.

(Check page 9 for the Addiction Scale)

CHILD ADDICTION

A common addiction is codependency. This includes, but is not limited to being addicted to people. Counselors, therapists and doctors often see many forms of this problem. This is when parents become dependent on their children to meet their adult emotional intimacy needs. Parents become enmeshed in their children's feelings, not recognizing whose feelings are whose. It is almost as though they cannot understand where one person begins and the other person ends emotionally. These parents may have a fear of abandonment or a poor sense of self, which can lead to an unhealthy need to unconsciously manipulate their children into altering their painful feelings.

Are you or someone you know addicted to a CHILD?

Those who are may:

☐ Have an out-of-control personal life because of a child.

☐ Be preoccupied with a child
(constantly talking or thinking about the child).

☐ Constantly be worrying over a child while at work or school.

☐ Frequently be suffering from insomnia because of a child.

☐ Be attempting to control a child (without reasonable cause).

☐ Be buying things for a child to gain his trust or love.

☐ Do things for a child who is capable of doing for himself.

☐ Have trouble in their primary relationships because of a child.

☐ Continue to believe a child who has lost all credibility.

☐ Blame him/herself for most of a child's pain or misfortune.

☐ Feel like a bad parent and/or stepparent.

☐ Suffer emotional or physical illness because of a child.

(Check page 9 for the Addiction Scale)

CHOCOLATE ADDICTION

Chocolate Addiction is as American as apple pie. These people eat chocolate for the taste, the high, the caffeine and the social pressure. Chocolate has high visibility as a safe, fun, relaxing, energizing and okay thing to eat. However, anything eaten without moderation can be destructive and addictive. Chocolate has addictive qualities. Chocolate Addicts are not always overweight. Sometimes they will work out at a gym or spa for hours just to be able to eat more chocolate. Rarely will they go one day without consuming chocolate.

Are you or someone you know addicted to CHOCOLATE?

Those who are may:

☐ Crave chocolate at a particular time of day.

☐ Often use chocolate as a pick-me-up.

☐ Hide or sneak chocolate.

☐ Frequently feel guilty about eating chocolate.

☐ Stop eating chocolate to prove they can live without it.

☐ Suffer physical problems as a result of eating chocolate.

☐ Tolerate and/or deny unwanted weight gain from eating chocolate.

☐ Be preoccupied with eating chocolate.

☐ Always have a supply of chocolate around "just in case."

☐ Increase the intake of chocolate over time.

☐ Eat large amounts of chocolate in one sitting.

☐ Find that others are concerned over their consumption of chocolate.

(Check page 9 for the Addiction Scale)

CLEANING ADDICTION

Cleaning Addiction may be a close relative of Activity Addiction; however, Cleaning Addiction is a specific obsessive-compulsive behavior. One theory is that these people may be in constant internal turmoil. This may be a result of weeks, months or even years of unresolved emotional pain. A key to healing this pain is to enter into therapy and identify where it is coming from. Those living with this condition may be acting out the pain in several ways that will often appear in the form of an obsessive-compulsive disorder or addiction, such as cleaning. It is difficult to recognize or intervene on this addiction, as it appears to be a responsible characteristic rather than a problem.

Are you or someone you know addicted to CLEANING?

Those who are may:

☐ Clean places or things that don't require cleaning.

☐ Easily become irritated by others who are not as tidy.

☐ Vacuum or clean more than once a day.

☐ Feel a sense of control or relief after cleaning.

☐ Spend long periods of time cleaning one project.

☐ Make cleaning a priority over intimate relationships.

☐ Believe it's never clean enough.

☐ Clean until they are exhausted.

☐ Repeatedly inspect others' cleaning ability or tidiness.

☐ Be critical of others in a general sense.

☐ Be very self-critical about cleaning yet wish not to be.

☐ Enter into an altered state or "high" when cleaning.

(Check page 9 for the Addiction Scale)

COFFEE ADDICTION

Coffee Addiction differs from Caffeine Addiction. Coffee, depending on whether or not it is caffeine free, can possess two addictive elements, the caffeine and the ritual. This particular segment will focus mainly on the ritualistic aspect of Coffee Addiction. Here, one will notice a strong emphasis put on how often coffee is around rather than how the drink itself alters a person's mood. Many Coffee Addicts rely on having a cup in hand to feel emotionally safe. Like a good friend, they may bring along coffee everywhere they go. It is as though they feel lost without it. It may even become as important to have around as a close friend or spouse. These people may not realize the strong bond they have with coffee until after they give it up. When they do give it up, only then will they experience an emotional psychological withdrawal syndrome.

Are you or someone you know addicted to COFFEE?

Those who are may:

- ☐ Usually or always have coffee with them.
- ☐ Usually insist others drink coffee with them.
- ☐ Feel anxiety or fear when coffee is not nearby.
- ☐ Have a favorite cup or thermos that is important to them.
- ☐ Drink coffee even against medical advice.
- ☐ Have had close calls from drinking coffee while driving.
- ☐ Find that others comment on their preoccupation with coffee.
- ☐ Choose to be late for an appointment rather than not have coffee.
- ☐ Feel less comfortable in a conversation without coffee.
- ☐ Notice their coffee intake has increased greatly over the years.
- ☐ Need a cup of coffee to function in the morning.
- ☐ Have developed physical ailments as a result of drinking coffee.

(Check page 9 for the Addiction Scale)

COMPUTER ADDICTION

On the surface this seems to be a socially acceptable activity. The trick is to identify the Computer Addict, rather than the person who uses the computer out of necessity for work, school, occasional information, conversation or financial survival.

The computer addict is in a relationship with the machine and it's power. The computer is not simply a "tool" which one uses or a casual communication device. This is serious business! The Computer Addict is not simply a person who uses the technology, but rather he/she protects the machine as if it were a life-long friend or relative. It is a sick relationship that leads to isolation, loneliness, depression and resentment. The computer takes the place of intimate relationships and becomes the "fix" for all emotional problems.

Teenagers are in particular danger due to the electronic predators who surf the web seeking vulnerable victims. Teenagers who are Computer Addicts are in immediate need of parental interventions and treatment.

All the joking about Internet addiction etc. makes it very difficult to identify, access and assist the Computer Addict.

Are you or someone you know addicted to the COMPUTER?

Those who are may:

☐ Spend most of their time on or with the computer.

☐ Feel threatened without access to a computer.

☐ Have lost jobs, credibility or relationships as a result of computer involvement.

☐ Spend most of their $$ on computers, supplies or computer related items.

☐ Be in debt or trouble because of computer involvement.

☐ Discount human value do to computer involvement.

☐ Be obsessed in conversation and reading about computers.

☐ Often stay up all night on the computer.

☐ Become upset and/or serious if confronted with computer involvement.

☐ Deny, rationalize or minimize any ill effects from computer involvement.

☐ Argue in a relationship over computer involvement.

☐ Have developed many social fears since being involved with the computer.

(Check page 9 for the Addiction Scale)

CONTROL ADDICTION

This addiction refers to those who spend most of their time attempting to control others. They are very difficult for others to tolerate. One theory is that these people may have felt very unsafe as children. The only salvation was to fantasize being in control of an out-of-control situation. They may have experienced extreme fear of loss or abandonment by parents or other authority figures. This, in turn, may have been carried into their adult relationships. Continuing to carry this pain, they make constant attempts to control people, places and things around them in hopes of creating the illusion of self-control or safety. This, in turn, eases the fear of abandonment. These people usually feel out of control inside, yet to others they appear to be in control. Normally the only people who experience the real person here are very close friends or family members.

Are you or someone you know addicted to CONTROL?

Those who are may:

☐ Usually be angry and rarely express it, yet others sense it.

☐ Usually give directions to others.

☐ Have difficulty taking direction.

☐ Generally be suspicious of others.

☐ Often feel depressed or exhausted.

☐ Have several physical complaints.

☐ Have lost important relationships due to their attempts to control.

☐ Fear public transportation and/or groups of people.

☐ Plan vacations, parties, etc. unreasonably long in advance.

☐ Have a deep fear of being out of control.

☐ Have to have the last word.

☐ Go to any lengths to be "right" or in control.

(Check page 9 for the Addiction Scale)

CRISIS ADDICTION

Here people are usually involved in some explosive or potentially explosive situations. Sometimes referred to as "crisis junkies" these people seem to have a need to live in constant conflict. One theory is that they may be acting out internal emotional turmoil that may have been brewing for years. Additionally, they may have been exposed to constant crisis as children and, since then, have become comfortable in a crisis. The problem is, those around them are violated by this behavior. This, in turn, creates a lifestyle of loneliness for these people because others eventually leave them to avoid the constant crises in their lives. Loneliness is particularly painful for these people because they need others around them who can participate in the crises.

Are you or someone you know addicted to CRISIS?

Those who are may:

☐ Get excited rather than afraid in a crisis.

☐ Seem to be in a crisis at least weekly.

☐ Create crisis and feel remorseful yet continue anyway.

☐ Have close friends who are usually in crisis.

☐ Regularly watch crisis oriented television programs.

☐ Look forward to the "adrenaline rush" from emergencies.

☐ Have lost relationships due to constant crisis.

☐ Have relationships that are usually exhausting.

☐ Be intrigued by accidents and others' misfortunes.

☐ Have great difficulty relaxing.

☐ Have become numb or immune to accidents, crisis, etc.

☐ Have a lifestyle that is usually or always high stress.

(Check page 9 for the Addiction Scale)

CULT ADDICTION

This is an addiction that is intended to relieve internal conflict by people becoming dependent on something outside themselves. These people rely 100% on outside influences for emotional and, many times, physical well being. In a form of institutionalization these people become prisoners in the cult. They lose the ability to determine personal rights or abilities becoming "other rated" and suffering from loss of self. They may develop a love-hate relationship with the cult. The cult may or may not be of a religious belief. It may be a group of individuals who have a strong belief in someone or something and then become willing to put everything and everyone on the line for it. This cult may be antisocial, illegal, immoral or anti-Christ. These addicts may also be victims of direct brainwashing.

Are you or someone you know addicted to CULTS?

Those who are may:

☐ Belong to a cult or cult-like organization.

☐ Feel out of control without the cult's direction.

☐ Do illegal or immoral things for the cult.

☐ Keep cult activities a secret.

☐ Have attended and/or participated in sacrifices.

☐ Feel afraid of the cult but participate fearing abandonment.

☐ Fear being alone.

☐ Define/identify themselves as the group rather than an individual.

☐ Find that others are concerned over this behavior.

☐ Have been arrested as a result of cult activities.

☐ Put others' lives in danger in order to participate in the cult.

☐ Experience reoccurring morbid thoughts and/or nightmares.

(Check page 9 for the Addiction Scale)

DANGER ADDICTION

This is an addiction that, many times, is encouraged by society and peer pressure. Those suffering from Danger Addiction take unreasonable risks to meet a need that cannot be met by human interaction. Often these people have a need to harm themselves or threaten their own lives. Some theories profess that these people had been abused as children, feel as if they are worth less than others and believe they deserve to be terrorized. On the surface, these people may appear quite rational, yet underneath it all, they cannot stand the status quo. They rarely feel complete as people or in touch with physical/emotional sensations unless putting their lives in danger.

Are you or someone you know addicted to DANGER?

Those who are may:

☐ Take unreasonable risks, putting themselves or others in danger.

☐ Find that others have continually expressed concern over this behavior.

☐ Have had many close calls, but it didn't deter the behavior.

☐ Find that others fear riding along in a car.

☐ Find that thrill rides are rarely stimulating anymore.

☐ Work in a dangerous profession (police, fireman, etc.).

☐ Find that others call them crazy.

☐ Be addicted to the "adrenaline rush."

☐ Thrive on threats.

☐ Be preoccupied with new ways to frighten themselves or others.

☐ Ignore danger signs or warnings posted by public officials.

☐ Have suffered physical injury due to dangerous encounters.

(Check page 9 for the Addiction Scale)

DEPRESSION ADDICTION

Depression may be a disease in itself. It may also be anger turned inward. Depression is a state of being rather than a specific feeling. It is when people feel a deep sadness for extended periods of time. Addictive depression is when people are in this state of being for long periods of time and deny it or never seem to have a desire to work through it. One thought is that these people get some sort of reward out of being depressed, such as attention from others or a sense of pity (others feeling sorry for them). It could be that they are acting out repressed pain from earlier years, childhood perhaps. In any case, they are unable to communicate with others and tell them what they really feel.

Are you or someone you know addicted to DEPRESSION?

Those who are may:

☐ Have many physical complaints yet refuse to see a doctor.

☐ Regularly suffer from insomnia.

☐ Eat to medicate their feelings.

☐ Become accustomed to feeling suicidal.

☐ Have the symptoms but deny being depressed.

☐ Use depression to avoid friends and family.

☐ Have sought professional help but stopped it prematurely.

☐ Find that others have given up on the situation.

☐ Feel that depression has become normal.

☐ Enjoy the attention given by others who are concerned about them.

☐ Be pessimistic about most things.

☐ Seek help yet never follow the advice.

(Check page 9 for the Addiction Scale)

DETAIL ADDICTION

This type of addiction is very irritating to others. These people seem to be angry and critical of others most of the time. They are perfectionists and have a need to get everything correct, right down to a gnat's eyebrows. This is highly obsessive-compulsive behavior. One theory is that these people will focus on detail in an effort to avoid undesirable feelings. The detail is always externally focused. One example would be compulsively looking for mistakes, (made by others of course) even the tiniest of errors, or making a big deal out of a minor part of an agreement, so much so that the agreement never gets solidified.

Are you or someone you know addicted to DETAIL?

Those who are may:

☐ Be a perfectionist most of the time.

☐ Put off finishing a project for minor reasons.

☐ Be very critical of others.

☐ Feel ashamed of others who represent or mirror them.

☐ Be rigid or resistant about most things.

☐ Insist on being detailed about insignificant things.

☐ Find that others are usually frustrated by this constant behavior.

☐ Have thoughts that they are too rigid or detailed.

☐ Feel incomplete as individuals without having everything in place.

☐ Silently correct or take inventory of professionals' work.

☐ Spend hours on simple projects.

☐ Keep detailed lists of things.

(Check page 9 for the Addiction Scale)

DIETING ADDICTION

This is a common problem, not to be confused with Eating Addiction, in which one has a compulsion to eat or not eat. This is about fixating on the process of dieting. People are looking for the quick fix and will go to any lengths to get it! Many have tried numerous diets. Some of these people really don't have an internalized desire to lose weight (even when they know they need to) but rather use the diet as a diversion from dealing with the real problem of unresolved emotional pain. Those who become addicted to dieting lose the original goal of losing weight. They become fixated on the process of dieting.

Are you or someone you know addicted to DIETING?

Those who are may:

☐ Be more concerned with the diet than weight loss.

☐ Try every new method available never sticking to one.

☐ Stop most diets prematurely.

☐ Find that others are tired of hearing about their diets.

☐ Diet to avoid intimacy (closeness with others).

☐ Lose control in other areas of their lives due to dieting.

☐ Feel like failures with dieting.

☐ Regularly cheat on diets and blame the diet for poor results.

☐ Take speed or illegal diet pills to diet.

☐ Spend large amounts of money on unsuccessful diets.

☐ Constantly talk about dieting.

☐ Argue with others over diets/dieting.

(Check page 9 for the Addiction Scale)

DRAMA ADDICTION

This process indicates an overwhelming need to draw attention to oneself by means of overemphasizing or dramatizing a problem, person or situation. Those suffering from Drama Addiction are often referred to as "Drama Queens". They will sometimes embarrass others by acting out antics. One theory is that, as children, these people had caregivers that viewed life as seriously overwhelming. Their parents blew routine, daily situations out of proportion creating an illusion for them that most things are overwhelming. It is also possible that these people come from very large families and had to be theatrical to gain attention. Whatever the case, these people are generally viewed by others as going overboard or making mountains out of molehills. People rarely take them seriously.

Are you or someone you know addicted to DRAMA?

Those who are may:

☐ Have an unrealistic perception of the world.

☐ Take most situations too seriously.

☐ Lie about things they did in order to create a dramatic story.

☐ Find that their public actions are embarrassing to others.

☐ At times, forget things they did while acting out.

☐ Plan out dramatic scenes to gain attention.

☐ Need to be the focus at social functions.

☐ Make dramatic entrances or exits at social events.

☐ Overreact to everyday problems or situations.

☐ Conduct detailed, boring conversations with others.

☐ Lose control while dramatizing (faint, etc.).

☐ Solicit others' attention/involvement in the acting out.

(Check page 9 for the Addiction Scale)

DRUG ADDICTION
(Prescription)

This form of drug addiction is the most covert form. Millions of people are addicted to prescription medications. Most deny the addiction via rationalization (e.g., "I'm not an addict. My doctor prescribed this for me."). Many become dependent on the mood altering effect; others become psychologically dependent on the security of believing that the drug will make them okay. The drug does not necessarily have to be mood altering. Drugs such as prescription strength aspirin, non-physically addictive psychiatric medication, birth control pills, etc. can all create a belief after a period of time that people cannot/ should not function without them. This is addiction. Some people take medication for years, yet never consider asking the doctor to decrease the dosage or take them off of it entirely.

Are you or someone you know addicted to PRESCRIPTION DRUGS?

Those who are may:

☐ Be taking prescription medication for a year or more.

☐ Have lied to the doctor about symptoms in order to get drugs.

☐ Take medication against medical advice.

☐ Go to more than one doctor with the goal of getting drugs.

☐ Feel great fear or panic when running low on or out of drugs.

☐ Lie to others about their drug use.

☐ Feel irritated toward others who have expressed concern.

☐ Feel ashamed of the drug use but continue anyway.

☐ Use the drug for emotional security (non-medical reasons).

☐ Feel agitated or angry without the drug.

☐ Defend the drug use.

☐ Think there may be a problem with their drug use.

(Check page 9 for the Addiction Scale)

DRUG ADDICTION
(Street Drugs)

This section includes all illicit drugs including, but not limited to marijuana, speed, cocaine, hash, LSD, PCP, morphine, heroin, mescaline, opium, glue sniffing, barbiturates, methadone, etc. When people become addicted to street substances, they become addicted to the mood or mind altering effect, not necessarily to that particular drug itself. They become "cross-addicted" switching from one drug to another in an effort to get away from or cease using a particular drug. The problem is that these people continue to need to alter their moods, making abstinence the furthest thing from their minds. If one knows someone addicted to a particular drug, he shouldn't believe they are clean or sober simply because they stopped using that particular drug. Abstinence from ALL drugs, including alcohol, is the only healthy or real form of recovery.

Are you or someone you know addicted to STREET DRUGS?

Those who are may:

☐ Experience personality changes when they use drugs.

☐ Experience trouble with the law because of drug use.

☐ Sell drugs or deal drugs to others.

☐ Find that drugs have become more important than friends or loved ones.

☐ Regret actions taken while under the influence.

☐ Lie to get drugs or money for drugs.

☐ Damage their job or school life by their drug use.

☐ Neglect other responsibilities because of drug use.

☐ Experience psychological or medical problems from drug use.

☐ Lose friends due to their involvement with drugs.

☐ Spend most of their money on drugs.

☐ Think there is a problem with their drug use.

(Check page 9 for the Addiction Scale)

EATING ADDICTION
(Overeating)

This particular addiction is not the disease of anorexia or bulimia. The focus here will be to cover specific symptoms of overeating. Anorexia and bulimia are diseases possessing their own particular characteristics and processes. Anorexia could be considered under-eating or starvation. Bulimia is characterized by overeating and then vomiting, better know as "binging and purging." One theory of overeating is that when people eat to excess, they are "stuffing their feelings" or repressing emotionally painful life issues. This becomes an addictive process. They must continue to eat to stuff feelings. As the pain becomes greater, the eating is more frequent and out of control. This is a vicious cycle of shame they must tolerate, making day-to-day life an emotionally exhausting nightmare for the afflicted.

Are you or someone you know addicted to EATING?

Those who are may:

☐ Be preoccupied with eating (thinking about it or planning it).

☐ Eat to help ease depression and/or stress.

☐ Be excessively overweight.

☐ Panic in social/recreational events without food around.

☐ Eat large amounts that others would consider abnormal.

☐ Feel guilty about personal eating habits.

☐ Eat when they're not hungry.

☐ Cheat on diets.

☐ Eat alone to hide how much they consume.

☐ Experience physical problems due to overeating.

☐ Hide food and feel ashamed about it.

☐ Find that their self-esteem is poor/suffering as a result of an eating problem.

(Check page 9 for the Addiction Scale)

EMOTIONAL ADDICTION

This section will address Emotional Addiction in general. Other sections of this book may focus on specific feelings such as mad, sad, glad, afraid, ashamed or hurt. Here, people may experience addiction to several feelings depending upon the situation. A person may become socially inappropriate and/or out of control emotionally due to this addiction. These people are usually out of balance with the rest of their reality, such as their thinking processes. To have ideal spiritual health they should be balanced emotionally, physically, intellectually, socially and spiritually. Emotional Addicts are overwhelmed by feelings. Even at times when it is best or more appropriate to conduct them selves intellectually, they may respond in emotional outbursts. Emotional Addicts have very little sense of this or the problems it may cause.

Are you or someone you know addicted to EMOTIONS?

Those who are may:

☐ Always respond to others out of feelings without thinking first.

☐ Feel emotionally overwhelmed a good deal of the time.

☐ Have emotional outbursts that cause problems at work.

☐ Often have emotional outbursts at home.

☐ Experience self-pity a great deal of the time.

☐ Be typically dissatisfied at not getting emotional responses from others.

☐ Usually be on an emotional roller coaster.

☐ Find that others usually have difficulty dealing with them.

☐ Have difficulty processing thoughts due to overwhelming emotion.

☐ Cry for long periods of time for unknown reasons.

☐ Feel "high" when experiencing most feelings.

☐ Have lost friends because of emotional outbursts.

(Check page 9 for the Addiction Scale)

EXERCISE ADDICTION

Many take offense to this one! Most workout addicts will fight to no end about this. There was even a book written entitled Positive Addiction, a book about running. I believe exercise is a necessary part of our physical and emotional well-being. Exercise Addiction is about lack of balance in critical aspects of the lives of those afflicted. It's also about using exercise to avoid emotional problems or intimacy. For instance, if one's intimate relationship suffers or is threatened because of exercise (always at the gym, never home) this is a problem. These people may be using exercise to avoid intimacy. Another problem arises when they are so preoccupied with exercise that they put off other significant responsibilities, e.g., work, parenting, rest, etc.

Are you or someone you know addicted to EXERCISE?

Those who are may:

☐ Exercise even if physical injury is present.

☐ Be irritable toward others when missing an exercise session.

☐ Have unreasonable fear of illness if not exercising.

☐ Think about exercising throughout the day, everyday.

☐ Exercise to the point that it interferes with other significant parts of their lives.

☐ Feel incomplete unless exercising to exhaustion each time.

☐ Be obsessed with their bodies.

☐ Believe, "If I am physically okay, everything is okay."

☐ Keep a rigid exercise schedule even in emergencies.

☐ Exercise to escape rather than relieve emotional issues.

☐ Feel obsessed to exercise more and more without relief.

☐ Have been advised to slow down or stop but can't.

(Check page 9 for the Addiction Scale)

EXHIBITIONISM ADDICTION

Exhibitionists are in violation of others' rights and boundaries. They lack a sense of social norms, or they ignore/deny them as a result of a compulsive need to exhibit themselves. This may be a result of being exposed and/or shamed as a child, creating a belief that they are not entitled to privacy or just not worthy as human beings. Exposing themselves may be an attempt at unloading their shame. On the other hand, they may have internalized emotional secrets that are eating away at them, and the only way to express them is by physical exhibition. Whatever the case, the Exhibitionism Addict is in deep emotional trouble.

Are you or someone you know addicted to EXHIBITIONISM?

Those who are may:

☐ Have a need to show off their bodies.

☐ Be arrested for exhibitionism.

☐ Get excited by shocking others with nudity.

☐ Flash others in public or socially unacceptable places.

☐ Spend as much time as possible in the nude.

☐ Answer the door in the nude.

☐ Be nude in socially unacceptable places or situations.

☐ Belong to a nudist colony.

☐ Lose friends because of exhibitionism.

☐ Ignore others' requests or needs around this issue.

☐ Have no sense of others' discomfort and/or don't care.

☐ Be generally offensive to others, and may also be arrogant.

(Check page 9 for the Addiction Scale)

FEAR ADDICTION

There are two ways to be addicted to fear, a need to have it or a need to avoid it. Either way, people's lives will revolve around fear when they become addicted to fear. In this section we will focus on symptoms that may apply to either.

Are you or someone you know addicted to FEAR?

Those who are may:

☐ Seek danger in almost everything.

☐ Make most decisions based on fear.

☐ Feel fear as their primary emotion; they feel other emotions only vaguely.

☐ Progress from fear to paranoia over a period of time.

☐ Be suspicious of almost everyone and everything.

☐ Not be able to imagine life without constant fear.

☐ Be constantly drawn to scary events or movies.

☐ Lose control in important areas of life because of fear.

☐ Have difficulty relaxing, and when they do, they worry that it won't last.

☐ Experience memory lapses at times during fearful incidents.

☐ Be a subject of concern to others because of their fear or paranoia.

☐ Avoid getting professional help for their fear.

(Check page 9 for the Addiction Scale)

FOOD ADDICTION

Different from Eating Addiction, although a very close relative, Food Addiction is more specifically about the ingestion of food rather than the ritual of eating. However, many symptoms may be overlapping. It is generally believed that Food Addiction is an escape from feelings; similar to the way an alcoholic drinks to avoid reality or undesirable feelings.

Are you or someone you know addicted to FOOD?

Those who are may:

- [ ] Eat to avoid or medicate feelings.
- [ ] Have self-esteem that is tied into cooking or food.
- [ ] Keep a supply of food around "just in case."
- [ ] Be grossly overweight.
- [ ] Feel ashamed of their food intake.
- [ ] Plan meals further in advance than necessary.
- [ ] Sneak or hide food.
- [ ] Regularly order or cook more food than is necessary.
- [ ] Suppress their appetites for only an hour or so by eating.
- [ ] Blame others for unhealthy eating habits.
- [ ] Generally hold conversations about food.
- [ ] Have friends or relatives who are concerned about their food intake.

(Check page 9 for the Addiction Scale)

GAMBLING ADDICTION

This is a very serious condition, not only for addicts, but for their families as well. Gambling Addicts become engulfed in gambling and blind to the consequences. It is like an alcoholic getting drunk and waking up in jail not knowing how it happened. The adrenaline rush that they experience from gambling is worth the risk of losing everything. This is truly a mood altering activity. It is chronic, progressive and possibly fatal. Suicide is attempted by many Gambling Addicts in order to avoid harm or ridicule from others. In some cases, they are beaten or even killed for unpaid gambling debts, and their family members may also be threatened or harmed.

Are you or someone you know addicted to GAMBLING?

Those who are may:

☐ Spend all or most of their money on gambling.

☐ Lie about gambling habits and/or debts, etc.

☐ Get into serious trouble because of gambling.

☐ Miss work because of gambling.

☐ Argue with family members over gambling issues.

☐ Be preoccupied with gambling (obsessed).

☐ Have made previous attempts to quit without success.

☐ Increase the amount of time or money being gambled.

☐ Revolve most social activities around gambling.

☐ Harbor secret feelings of shame over gambling.

☐ Steal to get money for gambling or gambling debts.

☐ Lose friends and/or credibility because of gambling.

(Check page 9 for the Addiction Scale)

GANG ADDICTION

Those who have difficulty accepting or defending themselves are prime candidates for gangs. Gang Addicts possess a tremendous need for external validation and security. Gangs provide a family for people who lack trust, security or acceptance at home. This is not to say everyone in a gang is from a "bad" family.

When considering joining a gang, people usually see the desirable aspect of the gang and may dismiss or deny the problems of being a member, even if most activities are threatening or dangerous. One of the problems is that it may be difficult, and even dangerous, to attempt to quit a gang. The other problem is that they may develop a strong dependency on the gang. Once involved, gang members take on certain responsibilities and develop a loyalty that is as strong as, if not stronger than, their loyalty to their families. The problem is, they lose personal identity to the gang, forget who they are and become something rather than someone. Gang members may also be addicted to many things inside the gang as well as to the institution itself.

Are you or someone you know addicted to a GANG?

Those who are may:

☐ Need a gang to have an identity.

☐ Be loyal, even when loyalty is not warranted.

☐ Feel ashamed of gang activity but stay anyway.

☐ Decide to leave/quit yet never follow through.

☐ Give up most friends outside of the gang.

☐ Frequently find their lives in danger due to gang activity.

☐ Keep gang life secret from all others.

☐ Have been arrested for gang activity.

☐ Feel alone, even in the crowd.

☐ Abandon all personal dreams or goals for the gang.

☐ Do anything for the gang regardless of the consequences.

☐ Lose personal pride or self-esteem because of the gang.

(Check page 9 for the Addiction Scale)

GOLF ADDICTION

This sport, although innocent enough, has been the culprit in many an argument in households around the world. "Golf widows" are a common result of the tragedy of those who spend more intimate time with their 5 irons than with their spouses. This sport is equally addicting to men and women. They become obsessed with the game, making improvements, getting frustrated and just having fun. They have tremendous mood swings as a result of this game. Beware; the rest of their lives could be suffering greatly as a result of over involvement in this sport.

Are you or someone you know addicted to GOLF?

Those who are may:

☐ Have a spouse or others who complain about the time they spend golfing.

☐ Regularly skip work to go golfing.

☐ Spend money they shouldn't and/or don't have on golf.

☐ Buy the latest equipment, even if it's not really needed.

☐ Think about golf constantly.

☐ Often practice golf at work.

☐ Watch golf religiously on television, despite others' wishes.

☐ At least once a week, abandon other responsibilities for golf.

☐ Golf to avoid intimacy (closeness with others).

☐ Golf to avoid/resolve most problems and/or conflicts.

☐ Only express feelings on the golf course.

☐ Find that golf has damaged their jobs or relationships.

(Check page 9 for the Addiction Scale)

HEALTH FOOD ADDICTION

As with any healthy game, process or sport, too much of a good thing can be detrimental. Health Food Addicts are not sick from the food they eat; they get sick from the obsessive process in which they are engaged. For instance, if they are obsessed with taking vitamins, they may be very critical of others who don't take vitamins. This can lead to loss of friends from forcing their beliefs onto others, much like a Religious Addict who believes in only one process of faith - all others may go to Hell. Health Food Addiction is usually difficult to confront.

Are you or someone you know addicted to HEALTH FOOD?

Those who are may:

☐ Not dream of eating junk food.

☐ Judge others harshly who don't always eat healthy.

☐ Not be able to enjoy social events because of the food served.

☐ Feel ashamed even when thinking about eating unhealthy.

☐ Make critical comments about others' eating habits.

☐ Have eating habits that are offensive to others

☐ Appear to look unhealthy from eating so much health food.

☐ Have conversations that are nearly always centered on health food.

☐ Have other critical life areas that suffer due to health food obsession.

☐ Be labeled "health food junkies" by friends and relatives.

☐ Be physically obsessed with themselves, neglecting their emotional sides.

☐ Lose friends because of a health food obsession.

(Check page 9 for the Addiction Scale)

INSTITUTIONAL ADDICTION

This is a common addiction, though not viewed as such, better known as "institutionalization." This may include, but is not limited to: prison, the military, a seminary, a psychiatric hospital or any other long-term residential program or facility. Addicts become dependent upon the rules of an institution to govern their lives thus losing the ability to make their own personal decisions or take action without others' permission or validation. They may suffer from a "loss of self" when confined for a long period of time, whether voluntarily or involuntarily. After entering back into society, they will generally find a way back into the institution or a similar facility or situation after a short period of time. They have great difficulty functioning without the institution.

Are you or someone you know addicted to INSTITUTIONS?

Those who are may:

☐ Be confined at least twice for 6 to 12 consecutive months.

☐ Have difficulty making personal decisions.

☐ Use alcohol or drugs to cope with society.

☐ Usually be anti-social or anti-society.

☐ Cope poorly without constant supervision (age appropriate).

☐ Have difficulty handling minor day-to-day responsibilities.

☐ Resent authority yet have a driving need for it.

☐ Be self-defeating and/or have a need to be punished or controlled.

☐ Have a tremendous fear of social situations.

☐ Feel guilty a good portion of the time.

☐ Avoid or undermine personal responsibility.

☐ Have returned to institutions several times.

(Check page 9 for the Addiction Scale)

LYING ADDICTION

Lying is an extremely destructive addiction that will quickly destroy the lives of those addicted to it. Lying can be more socially unacceptable than drug use. Pathological liars, or Lying Addicts, are generally disliked or resented by others. There is an old adage, "If you tell the truth, you don't need a good memory." It is typical for Lying Addicts to forget the lies they have told. They generally have a tremendous need for acceptance and will go to any lengths to be validated by others. One theory is that they were reared in a family that rarely validated or supported anyone. They may have needed to lie to get attention or avoid abandonment. This, in turn, became an addictive vicious cycle for them as adults. Losing friends easily is a hallmark symptom of this addiction. Most people will not confront Lying Addicts about their dishonesty. Instead, they will generally turn their backs and just leave. Lying Addicts will eventually suffer from chronic depression or loneliness.

Are you or someone you know addicted to LYING?

Those who are may:

☐ Lie when it is just as easy to tell the truth.

☐ Feel in control when getting away with lying.

☐ Have an extreme fear of abandonment.

☐ Be highly suspicious or paranoid of others.

☐ Lie to cover lies.

☐ Forget the lies that have been told.

☐ Lose friends because of lying.

☐ Feel ashamed of constant lying but continue anyway.

☐ Lie under oath.

☐ Regularly lie to loved ones.

☐ Not be deterred from lying by the consequences.

☐ Find that lying has become physically exhausting.

(Check page 9 for the Addiction Scale)

MASTURBATION ADDICTION

A close relative of the Sex Addict, those addicted to masturbation are compelled to find an emotional release through physical sexual release. The problem is that they don't seek out healthy ways to release emotional, and sometimes physical, tension. As the problem progresses, they usually become more isolated and secretive. Many times they will invite or convince others to participate in the activity. The motivation behind the addiction is generally shame-based. Masturbation Addiction is rarely about sex. It represents more of an internal emotional struggle and, possibly, a fear of sexuality.

Are you or someone you know addicted to MASTURBATION?

Those who are may:

☐ Fear there may be something wrong with them.

☐ Masturbate several times a day.

☐ Masturbate at inappropriate places (work, school, etc.).

☐ Be disinterested in sex with others.

☐ Call sex phone lines on a regular basis.

☐ Think about masturbating much of the time.

☐ Masturbate to relieve emotional pain.

☐ Put off important tasks in order to masturbate.

☐ Feel overwhelmed with shame from masturbating.

☐ Make promises to themselves to stop but can't.

☐ Find that masturbating has caused problems in their relationships.

☐ Frequent adult bookstores or porno movies to masturbate.

(Check page 9 for the Addiction Scale)

We have an appointment at 9 with the Nutritionist, at 10 with Dr. Jones for my arthritis, at 11 with Dr. Smith for your feet, at noon we have the Brown Bag Lunch Seminar on "Home Safety for the Elderly", at 1 we have to get our eyes checked at Dr. Adams...

MEDICAL ADDICTION

Many people in American society have become addicted to medical assistance. The system is necessary for our well-being and it saves lives. The problem with Medical Addicts is that they rely heavily or solely on the medical system to survive emotionally as well as physically. Their lives become off balance due to overemphasis on and preoccupation with the medical system. They may cease to rely on friends, family, church or other important life sustaining elements. Medical Addicts are not balanced physically, spiritually, emotionally and intellectually. Their world becomes smaller and smaller as time goes on and they become more chronically involved with the medical system. They rely only on what the physician tells them, and they don't or can't listen to their own internal cues. This can be considered a codependent relationship with the medical system. Our senior citizens are more reliant on the system than other forms of healing, such as holistic or spiritual. This, however, seems to be changing. The managed care health system, by cutting costs, medical procedures and lengths of stay at hospitals, has shown the majority of people (but not all of them) just how addicted they have become to the medical system and how they abuse it.

Are you or someone you know addicted to the MEDICAL SYSTEM?

Those who are may:

☐ Have several physical complaints without medical diagnoses.

☐ Feel better or cured even on the way to the doctor.

☐ Be preoccupied with physical illness (obsessed).

☐ Own a personal P. D. R. (Physician's Desk Reference).

☐ Only feel safe or comfortable if medical help is nearby.

☐ Need to have medical procedures performed to feel okay.

☐ Be stuck in a pattern of seeing physicians without having a chronic illness.

☐ Spend most of their money on medical procedures/system.

☐ Constantly talk about the system or personal medical problems.

☐ Have a diminished sex drive or sex life because of medical preoccupation.

☐ Have friends or loved ones who are frustrated over constant medical procedures.

☐ Feel in a vicious circle or no-win situation medically.

(Check page 9 for the Addiction Scale)

MONEY ADDICTION

There are many of these addicts in our society. As a matter of fact, our society in general is addicted to money. Money becomes the quick fix for all problems, to Money Addicts. Their entire self-worth is based on $$$. Money is the first goal, the first priority and the first love. Money Addiction is much more self-destructive than Drug Addiction simply because it is not only accepted by society, but it is how many people value others in business and, many times, personal relationships. Money has probably destroyed more relationships than drugs have.

Are you or someone you know addicted to MONEY?

Those who are may:

☐ Never be able to get enough money.

☐ Lie to get money.

☐ Feel worthless as a person without money.

☐ Hide money from significant others.

☐ Cheat friends and/or relatives for money.

☐ Think about money 60% of the time.

☐ Lose friends because of money.

☐ Often fight with loved ones about money.

☐ Have money yet rarely spend it and be known as cheap.

☐ Violate their personal value system for money.

☐ Convey by their actions that money is more important than anything else.

☐ Use money to buy intimacy or fix things emotionally.

(Check page 9 for the Addiction Scale)

MUSIC ADDICTION

Music is a very powerful way of communicating. It is mood altering, making people vulnerable to becoming addicted to it. I will be so bold as to say that I believe Music Addiction is the most predominant addiction in the world. It is socially acceptable, pleasurable, healing - the list goes on. Why then is it unhealthy? Music itself is not unhealthy. It is when people become obsessed to the point that other life sustaining activities and relationships are harmed, put off or denied as a result of their relationship with music that it becomes unhealthy. Music Addicts will not be able to function for very long without music, or, when music is taken away, they will experience a type of withdrawal. Music Addicts will use music to avoid internal emotional pain rather than use the music to help process through the pain. It is difficult to identify a Music Addict because of widespread acceptance of the use of music everywhere. There are, however, some distinctive signs of a Music Addict.

Are you or someone you know addicted to MUSIC?

Those who are may:

☐ Listen to music nearly every waking hour.

☐ Have difficulty being alone or not be able to stand the quiet.

☐ Spend a major portion of their money on music.

☐ Use music to avoid intimacy.

☐ Allow significant areas of their lives to deteriorate because of music.

☐ Wear headphones as much as possible to tune out the world.

☐ Find that music has a negative effect on their performance at work or school.

☐ Suffer from insomnia without music.

☐ Only be able to express feelings through music, rarely through 3 conversation.

☐ Need music to feel.

☐ Spend more money on music than they can afford.

☐ Hear others complain about their preoccupation with music.

(Check page 9 for the Addiction Scale)

NEGATIVITY ADDICTION

Negativity Addicts have the philosophy that, "A pessimist is an optimist with experience." Negativity Addicts are easy to spot. They have something demeaning to say about anyone or anything. There is always a derogatory comment reflecting inner feelings about life. One theory is that Negativity Addicts had a very pessimistic parent during childhood. Common phrases heard in a pessimistic family are, "Where did you get a dumb idea like that," or "That will never work," or "I wish we could do that, but we know it's not possible." These people see life as a struggle rather than a journey; furthermore, they are emotionally draining to be around. They usually end up being alone.

Are you or someone you know addicted to NEGATIVITY?

Those who are may:

☐ Feel relief from others' failure.

☐ Frequently make negative remarks to or about others.

☐ Feel trapped in negative thoughts.

☐ Lose friends due to a negative attitude.

☐ Resent or distrust happy or positive people.

☐ Usually feel hopeless.

☐ Typically hold up a group's decision with pessimism.

☐ Seem to be victims much of the time.

☐ View everything as a problem as opposed to a challenge.

☐ Have low self-esteem because of constant negativity.

☐ Be suspicious of or question everything and everyone.

☐ Deny or minimize personal accomplishments.

(Check page 9 for the Addiction Scale)

NICOTINE ADDICTION

Nicotine, according to Webster's dictionary, is "a poisonous alkaloid that is the chief added principle in tobacco and is used as a pesticide." People become addicted to the mood altering effects of nicotine, a dangerous drug that is probably the number one killer in the United States. This drug is highly publicized and glorified in the Orient. It is socially acceptable worldwide (although its popularity is diminishing in the U.S.), making it a "sneaky drug" waiting to lure in younger people. Nicotine is a minor mood altering substance. People develop a tolerance to the chemical and increase their tobacco intake. Unlike Smoking Addiction, where people are also addicted to the ritual, here, they become physically addicted. The consequences are fatal in many cases.

Are you or someone you know addicted to NICOTINE?

Those who are may:

☐ Chew or smoke tobacco regularly.

☐ Crave nicotine at a certain time of day.

☐ Attempt to stop using nicotine/tobacco without success.

☐ Have physical problems as a result of nicotine intake.

☐ Experience withdrawal when stopping the use of nicotine/tobacco.

☐ Use more nicotine/tobacco now than a year ago.

☐ Know others who have expressed concern over their smoking/chewing tobacco.

☐ Use nicotine/tobacco to feel at ease at a social event.

☐ Have thoughts like "I may have a problem with nicotine/tobacco."

☐ Promise to quit yet never do so permanently.

☐ Sneak or hide nicotine/tobacco.

☐ Become angry or defensive when others discuss nicotine/tobacco use.

(Check page 9 for the Addiction Scale)

PAIN ADDICTION (PHYSICAL)

This is a problem in which the addicts have an unconscious need to feel physical discomfort much of the time. A couple of theories are that they were physically abused as children or that they witnessed an important person in their lives (their mother or father, for instance) suffer great, chronic physical pain (such as a long term chronic illness). They internalized or took on this person's emotional pain caused by the physical illness. Now, being that they were intimate with this other person during the period of chronic illness, this pain may show up during their adult life, particularly when they become intimate with another. The intimacy may remind them of their bond with the past significant other, their intimacy and that person's physical illness. This is a repeat pattern and will continue until some emotional/psychological work is done. Watch for when the symptoms occur and if there is any pattern around the time they become ill each time. That will be a key to discovering the core issue here.

Are you or someone you know addicted to PHYSICAL PAIN?

Those who are may:

☐ Focus private time on physical pain/discomfort.

☐ Often complain about physical pain yet rarely seek medical help.

☐ Compare their pain to others.

☐ Find that pain seems to be present during particular problems or situations.

☐ Not follow through on medical advice.

☐ Constantly look for something to be physically wrong.

☐ Use pain to gain attention.

☐ Use pain to avoid intimacy.

☐ Intentionally use pain to avoid responsibility.

☐ Work hard at convincing others of the physical pain.

☐ Never feel physical pain during select activities (shopping, sex, etc.).

☐ Find that many others believe their pain is psychological.

(Check page 9 for the Addiction Scale)

PARENT ADDICTION

Usually present in adults, this addiction causes difficulty in intimate relationships with others because the addicts have not broken free or made the shift from adolescence to adulthood. They remain bonded to a parent in an unhealthy or self-destructive way. One theory is that, as children, they felt responsible for one or both of their parents' wellbeing. They were enmeshed (bonded in an unhealthy way) to Mom or Dad. Their parent(s) didn't encourage a separation from childhood to adulthood because they had an unconscious need for the adolescent to carry their emotional pain. Another theory is that the children felt disloyal by leaving home. Their parent(s) did not support them by letting them know that it is natural to "leave the nest" and to experience pain and reservation over it. Parents with unmet emotional intimacy needs hang-on-to their children, crippling them emotionally for life. Even after their parents are dead and gone, the children will have this issue. People with this problem must seek professional help.

Are you or someone you know addicted to a PARENT?

Those who are may:

☐ Continue to live at home more than 2 years after becoming legal adults.

☐ Telephone parents daily to remind them they love and/or care about them.

☐ Feel guilty when not always including a parent in on their personal lives.

☐ Resent the bond with a parent yet fear addressing the problem.

☐ Damage intimate relationships because of the parental bond.

☐ Continue to take orders from the parent and resent it.

☐ Usually do for a parent what the parent is capable of doing for himself.

☐ Feel lost without a parent's direction.

☐ Need the parent to make or help make most personal decisions.

☐ Feel angry or depressed when around their parents.

☐ Give and give to the parent even when they rarely receive anything from the parent.

(Check page 9 for the Addiction Scale)

PERSON ADDICTION
(CODEPENDENCY)

As in Parent Addiction, codependency (better known as "loss of self") is the trait that characterizes an addiction to another person. Here, the addicts have a need to rely on another's validation in order to function. They may be addicted to several people or just one. These addicts lack boundaries. Boundaries represent a sense of self that is lacking with Person Addicts. They feel terror when alone once addicted to another person. One theory is that they have suffered from abandonment or some other type of abuse in which their instincts were questioned, damaged or denied. At this point, they have very little self-trust; therefore, they have to look outside of themselves and trust others more than themselves.

Are you or someone you know addicted to a PERSON?

Those who are may:

☐ Feel compelled to obey the person to avoid rejection or receive validation.

☐ Rely on the other person for self-worth.

☐ Feel abused by the other person yet don't confront the situation.

☐ Attempt to control the person and often feel frustrated.

☐ Say yes to the person when they want to say no.

☐ Distrust the person yet never speaks about it to him.

☐ Complain about the person to others but not to him.

☐ Always try to please the other person, neglecting his or her own needs.

☐ Fear abandonment from the person and be willing to do anything to hold on.

☐ Lie to the person, fearing the consequences for honesty.

☐ Feel the other person's pain more than their own.

☐ Blame the person for most of the problems in their lives.

(Check page 9 for the Addiction Scale)

PET ADDICTION

A common addiction that is rarely discussed is Pet Addiction. People addicted to their pets have a relationship with the pet that is obsessive. Others may become bored or angry listening to Pet Addicts' stories about their pets. One theory is that they fixate on the animal because they have little to say about themselves. Or, they may have an obsessive need to be caring for others. This may be a result of unmet childhood needs. This addiction goes beyond the natural nurturing of a pet; it may be an attempt to meet the addicts' unmet intimacy needs. Pets are not judgmental, and they will usually stay around under any circumstances. People may get emotionally close to their pets to avoid feelings of abandonment by human beings. This is not necessarily bad; however, if they rely on this constantly, their emotional intimacy needs may never be met in a healthy manner.

Are you or someone you know addicted to a PET?

Those who are may:

- [ ] Know others who have a sick relationship with a pet.
- [ ] View their pet as their child.
- [ ] Spend large quantities of money on non-essential items for a pet.
- [ ] Pay more attention to a pet than to their human relationships.
- [ ] Miss work/school or leave early for a pet.
- [ ] Worry over a pet 2 to 3 times a day.
- [ ] Overprotect or obsess about the pet.
- [ ] Cover up accidents for a pet (to keep the pet out of trouble).
- [ ] Sleep with a pet on a regular basis.
- [ ] Isolate a pet (keep it for themselves).
- [ ] Feel overwhelmingly responsible for a pet.
- [ ] Allow a pet to do whatever it wants, even if it violates others.

(Check page 9 for the Addiction Scale)

PHYSICAL ILLNESS ADDICTION

Here, people have a tremendous emotional need to be physically ill. When suffering from this type of addiction, they may only feel alive when they are sick. They relate to the world through physical illness. It is a physically, as well as emotionally, painful way to conduct life. Physical Illness Addicts grow accustomed to this state and may become immune to feeling minor illnesses. This makes for a dangerous pattern. Those with this problem will usually end up alone because it limits their ability to function on all life sustaining levels (physical, emotional, intellectual, sexual and spiritual) in a relationship. Partners in relationships with these addicts can only deal with them for so long before abandoning them out of frustration. Deep down these addicts don't want to get well. They may fear having the ability to relate to life any other way.

Are you or someone you know addicted to PHYSICAL ILLNESS?

Those who are may:

☐ Actively seek out yet fear new diseases.

☐ Experience physical illness 60% of the time or more.

☐ Visit the doctor frequently to rule out illness.

☐ Often fear their illness is fatal, without diagnosis.

☐ Constantly think about their physical health and illness.

☐ Have had several undiagnosed medical problems.

☐ Find that others have stopped believing them.

☐ Use more than their allotted sick leave at work.

☐ Lose jobs due to constant illness.

☐ Regularly enjoy the attention received when ill.

☐ Research illnesses they don't have.

☐ Find that intimacy with others have constantly suffered because of illness.

(Check page 9 for the Addiction Scale)

PITY ADDICTION

These people are usually looking for sympathy and will go to just about any lengths to get it. As children, their needs were probably met only when others sensed misfortune. It may have become a pattern for them in adulthood, to continue meeting their intimacy needs this way. They become a quick fix for someone else's ego that happens to be in the market for helping other unfortunates. The danger here is that Pity Addicts may get into a depression that is very difficult to reverse, simply because they are victims of their own sorrow.

Are you or someone you know addicted to PITY?

Those who are may:

- ☐ Often wonder, "Why me?"
- ☐ Seem to get all the bad breaks or bad luck.
- ☐ Usually hold conversations consisting of asking questions.
- ☐ Rarely make responsible statements ("I believe..." etc.).
- ☐ Often blame others for sadness or sorrow.
- ☐ Seek friends that have a need and/or want to fix others.
- ☐ Feel sad 60% of the time or more.
- ☐ Seem to be generally unlucky.
- ☐ Often drink over sorrow.
- ☐ Complain about "poor me" yet don't seek professional help.
- ☐ Feel misunderstood by most others.
- ☐ Be a scapegoat or target for others' anger or resentment.

(Check page 9 for the Addiction Scale)

PORNOGRAPHY ADDICTION

Pornography Addicts meet sexual needs with pornography. It is a safe way to feel sexual without a commitment to another person. They live life as hostages to guilt and shame. The major problem with this addiction is that it robs the victims of intimate sexual experiences with others. Many have reported failed marriages as a result of this addiction. In relationships, they may need pornography to get "turned on" or as foreplay, and they are unable to function without it. This is damaging to the entire relationship in that it may be insulting to their partners when they constantly have to use pornography in order to engage in sexual activity. On the other hand, Pornography Addicts may avoid intimate relationships altogether as a result of their dependence on pornography.

Are you or someone you know addicted to PORNOGRAPHY?

Those who are may:

☐ Subscribe to or regularly purchase pornographic magazines.

☐ Regularly attend pornographic movies.

☐ Frequent adult bookstores or sex arcades.

☐ Feel ashamed over personal sexual behavior.

☐ Spend great effort hiding their obsession.

☐ Lie about pornographic activities or the obsession.

☐ Feel out of control or acknowledge the need for help.

☐ Swear off pornographic involvement at one time or another.

☐ Embarrass others with pornographic discussions.

☐ Engage in making pornographic films.

☐ Put off important tasks to participate in pornographic activity.

☐ Have been arrested on pornography related charges.

(Check page 9 for the Addiction Scale)

POWER ADDICTION

Many with this addiction feel out of control or powerless. They seem to have a need to be above others in order to feel adequate as human beings. They are perceived as arrogant, obnoxious or shameless. Many of these people are high achievers, possibly addicted to achievement because they fear failure. They may have difficulty relaxing or being with people because they don't know how to socialize. They are caught up in performing well. One theory is that these addicts never felt adequate as children. Their parent(s) or caregivers rarely acknowledged any accomplishments. Worse yet, jealous parents may have shamed them for their achievements. Whatever the case, they may become suicidal or isolated as a result of the chronic effects of this addiction.

Are you or someone you know addicted to POWER?

Those who are may:

- ☐ Put down or shame others on a regular basis.
- ☐ Do whatever it takes to win an argument.
- ☐ Emotionally harm others in an effort to control them.
- ☐ Rarely, if ever, apologize.
- ☐ Have a strong need for praise.
- ☐ Be feared or distrusted by others.
- ☐ Fear failure.
- ☐ Lack humility (the ability to be wrong, take advice, etc.).
- ☐ Lie to cover up normal human problems to appear strong.
- ☐ Constantly view others' feelings as weak.
- ☐ Feel terrified within.
- ☐ Rage at or lose patience with others when they don't get their own way.

(Check page 9 for the Addiction Scale)

PROCRASTINATION ADDICTION

These people are experts at putting things off. They don't seem to care about others' time or feelings. "Excuse" is their middle name. "Why do it today when you can put it off until tomorrow" is their motto. Procrastinators are usually angry or frustrated, and procrastination may be a way of indirectly expressing that anger. They apologize so much that nobody believes the apologies anymore. Another characteristic of Procrastination Addicts is always being over scheduled or having more projects than they can handle. They rarely finish things. Furthermore, as long as they are busy or overbooked, it is difficult for them to focus on the here and now, so they are able to avoid unpleasant circumstances, responsibilities or feelings. Others rarely feel heard, respected or validated by these people.

Are you or someone you know addicted to PROCRASTINATION?

Those who are may:

☐ Be late at least 50% of the time.

☐ Have a vocabulary made up of excuses.

☐ Have lost credibility with others due to tardiness.

☐ Feel frustrated with themselves much of the time.

☐ Be avoided by others.

☐ Be unable to sense or respond to others' frustration.

☐ Lose jobs, accounts or friends due to procrastination.

☐ Find that their procrastination has gotten worse over time.

☐ Usually be in a hurry attempting to catch up or make up.

☐ Feel unmotivated 50% of the time.

☐ Rarely finish tasks or assignments.

☐ Deny and/or minimize the consequences of procrastination.

(Check page 9 for the Addiction Scale)

PROFANITY ADDICTION

Profanity is sometimes referred to as "swearing." Profanity Addicts may be frustrated and feel others don't hear them. They may believe that one way to get others' attention or shock them is to swear. These people may have been raised in an environment where swearing or profanity was used daily. Nevertheless, it is socially unacceptable behavior and creates emotional distance between people. Profanity Addicts are harmful to others. They offend people, not realizing the damage that is being done. Only when it is too late do Profanity Addicts realize the destruction done by their language. They usually end up being alone or harshly judged as bad people due to their constant swearing. Others are intimidated by foul language and try to avoid these people. Profanity Addicts lack boundaries or rules that help them recognize others' rights and feelings when it comes to communication.

Are you or someone you know addicted to PROFANITY?

Those who are may:

- [ ] Usually use profanity to express anger or frustration.
- [ ] Swear unconsciously.
- [ ] Use language that is embarrassing to others in social settings.
- [ ] Use profanity to control or intimidate others.
- [ ] Have a desire to stop swearing but can't
- [ ] Feel frustrated with themselves and be short-tempered.
- [ ] Call friends or loved ones vulgar names.
- [ ] Rarely make a statement without profanity.
- [ ] Have been in trouble several times due to swearing.
- [ ] Swear at socially unacceptable places (church, school, etc.).
- [ ] Feel ashamed over their use of profanity.
- [ ] Have "sexualized rage" or frustration over their sex lives.

(Check page 9 for the Addiction Scale)

PROSTITUTION ADDICTION

This particular addiction refers to those who are prostitutes as opposed to those who hire prostitutes. They usually begin this behavior innocently (as with most addictions). The initial reward is fast money. The problem continues as their self-esteem declines as a result of their involvement in demoralizing acts. The prostitutes generally rationalize this by thinking "it's just a job. I'm not involved." Many immediate life-threatening problems are present with this addiction, sexually transmitted diseases for one. Prostitutes may rationalize or deny the risks involved. They may even be able to minimize the physical risk. However, they always "sell out" their own value systems or self-esteem as a result of involvement in this addiction.

Are you or someone you know addicted to PROSTITUTION?

Those who are may:

☐ Get their primary income from prostitution.

☐ Feel ashamed and hide this activity from loved ones.

☐ Have been in physical danger from selling sex; yet continue to do so.

☐ Feel worthless or abused yet continue prostitution.

☐ Feel guilty about involvement in prostitution.

☐ Have friends who are involved in sexual exploitation.

☐ Constantly defend the actions of prostitution.

☐ Make personal commitments to stop but break their promises.

☐ Have been arrested for prostitution, which doesn't deter them.

☐ Have difficulty/inability maintaining a relationship due to prostitution.

☐ Live in fear or paranoia because of prostitution.

☐ Lose most of their decent friends because of prostitution.

(Check page 9 for the Addiction Scale)

READING ADDICTION

Reading is a seemingly harmless activity, even healthy most of the time; yet it has potentially addictive qualities. People addicted to reading are usually "buried" in a book. They avoid reality by reading. They may lack social skills and find reading a safe place to hide out. The problem lies in the fact that these people are not balanced in all areas of reality (i.e., emotional, intellectual, social, physical and spiritual). Their lives are engulfed in an isolated world of paper and ink. Others may feel isolated from or ignored by these people as well. Reading may be used as a replacement for intimacy. Reading Addicts may suffer from chronic loneliness.

Are you or someone you know addicted to READING?

Those who are may:

☐ Use reading to escape responsibilities.

☐ Hide books at work to read.

☐ Spend almost all their free time reading.

☐ Often isolate themselves from others to be able to read.

☐ Buy books for their "emergency" supply.

☐ Neglect significant others to read.

☐ Attempt to cut back on reading without success.

☐ Feel lost without a book.

☐ Be thought by others to read too much.

☐ Be preoccupied with reading, even while doing other things.

☐ Often read to avoid intimacy.

☐ Usually read to avoid feelings.

(Check page 9 for the Addiction Scale)

RELATIONSHIP ADDICTION

This is probably one of the most destructive addictions of all. It is a common term used to describe codependency. Relationship Addiction is an emotional disease. One theory is that people suffering from this addiction were raised to depend so much on others that they are unable to function without others' validation. As a wise old adage goes, "Give a man a fish, you feed him for a day. Teach a man to fish, you feed him for life." Relationship Addicts were taught dependency rather than autonomy. Over the years, they have become terrified of abandonment. They may become addicted in a dysfunctional relationship yet can't leave due to fear of being alone. Without professional intervention, these people may never get out of the relationship and may become spiritually bankrupt and die emotionally. These people develop a tolerance to abuse that may be unbelievable to others, withstanding the deepest of emotional, and possibly physical, abuse from another person.

Are you or someone you know addicted to a RELATIONSHIP?

Those who are may:

☐ Stay in a relationship that is physically or emotionally abusive.

☐ Drop most of their friends for the relationship.

☐ Be obsessed with the relationship and feel sick from it.

☐ Spend hours in grief or pain over the relationship everyday.

☐ Give and give but rarely receive in the relationship.

☐ Blame the other person for most of their problems.

☐ Often have others express concern over the relationship.

☐ Request help or support from others, only to reject it.

☐ Often suffer at work or school over the relationship.

☐ Distrust the other person involved and fear abandonment.

☐ Feel like a hostage in the relationship with no way out.

☐ Feel terror when thinking about leaving the relationship.

(Check page 9 for the Addiction Scale)

RELIGIOUS ADDICTION

Let me begin by saying that most people that have a strong faith do so in a way that attracts others to participate in their particular faith. Religious Addicts usually do not attract people but rather they offend them. This is an addiction of boundary deficiency. Here, addicts become so obsessed with religion that they may attempt to educate or recruit others without sensing their reservations about or frustration with being educated or recruited. Religious Addicts generally hide behind their belief in a particular religion and, in fact, rarely practice what they preach. These people are notorious for violating others' boundaries (personal rights). Their religion becomes a vehicle to avoid taking responsibility for their own lives. Religion itself is healthy and necessary; however, people who are entirely obsessed have lost faith; that is, if they ever had any to begin with. Important areas of their lives suffer as a result of their religious practices (relationship, work, school, etc.). These addicts are usually very rigid and controlling, not allowing for spontaneity in their lives. When people abandon their spontaneity, they may be spiritually dead anyway.

Are you or someone you know addicted to RELIGION?

Those who are may:

☐ Generally "turn off" others with religion.

☐ Insist on their religious belief being the only way.

☐ Attempt to "save" others whether they want it or not.

☐ Not practice what they preach.

☐ Attend church daily, relying on absolutely nothing else.

☐ Use prayer to fix all problems without taking personal action.

☐ Become more rigid about religion over time.

☐ Often stop strangers to preach the gospel.

☐ Lack a sense of others' boundaries, personal rights, and beliefs.

☐ Contribute nearly all their money to the church.

☐ Lose friends over religion and their rigidity about it.

☐ Read material pertaining only to their religion.

(Check page 9 for the Addiction Scale)

SADNESS ADDICTION

Not to be confused with Depression Addicts, although close relatives, Sadness Addicts seem to get their needs met by being sad much of the time. They may use sadness to manipulate others; however, it may eventually turn into a chronic addiction. One theory is that these people were exposed to care givers who had enormous unresolved grief. As children, these people observed the attention their caregivers received for having all this sadness, enforcing an idea that, in order to receive or deserve attention, they must be sad. Another theory is that these people have a tremendous amount of unresolved grief and are caught up in a vicious cycle of attempting to debrief or divulge the grief over and over, never finding an effective way of releasing it. These people need to enter professional therapy to assist in resolving this emotional problem. A Sadness Addict is very difficult for others to tolerate. This behavior generally results in deterioration of personal relationships and loneliness for addicts, which, in turn, perpetuates the sadness.

Are you or someone you know addicted to SADNESS?

Those who are may:

☐ Feel lonely most of the time.

☐ Listen to sad songs, even when they already feel depressed.

☐ Often receive attention or validation when they feel sad.

☐ Feel safe or familiar when sad.

☐ Experience sadness that goes on for days, without attempting to stop it (self-pity).

☐ Attempt to get professional help but stop prematurely.

☐ Find others avoiding them in an attempt to avoid sad stories.

☐ Often feel hopeless and accept it as a part of life.

☐ Have difficulty having fun and rarely smile.

☐ Have crying jags on command or for no reason at all.

☐ Generally view life as dull.

☐ Often wallow in self-pity, expecting others to feel sad, too.

(Check page 9 for the Addiction Scale)

SCHOOL ADDICTION

"Professional students" are those whose lives are centered on school. This addiction is more recognizable in adults since, for children, school really is their primary job. This addiction does not exclude children. These people may also be Reading Addicts. People that have been in junior college for over three years and have not obtained an Associate's Degree are a tip-off. In children or adolescents, if their social calendar is empty a good portion of the time, this may be a clue. For whomever this problem exists, the destructiveness is in the obsession. One theory is that these people have not adapted social skills or self-esteem high enough to participate on a comfortable level in social settings or, quite possibly, in intimate one-on-one settings. School Addicts are usually intelligent people and rate high on the intellectual scale yet rate low on emotional and social scales.

Are you or someone you know addicted to SCHOOL?

Those who are may:

☐ Use school to avoid other personal problems.

☐ Spend extended periods of time at school.

☐ Neglect other responsibilities to attend school.

☐ Spend an unreasonable amount of income on school.

☐ Constantly talk about school.

☐ Regularly overextend themselves in school.

☐ Attend school to escape crisis or other stress.

☐ Make others feel abandoned or neglected because of school.

☐ Have attended college for 4 years without obtaining a degree.

☐ Always put school before family or other loved ones.

☐ Abandon all social life because of school.

☐ Be defensive of others who express concerned about their school obsession.

(Check page 9 for the Addiction Scale)

SEMINAR ADDICTION

Also known as "seminar junkies," these people may be looking for a guru to tell them what to do, how to live life or, possibly, who they are. Seminar Addicts are searching for an external fix. They don't seem to grow emotionally but may attend seminars to avoid making personal changes. By attending seminars, they appear to be making an effort to change or improve. The problem is that they rarely make any internal changes. Seminar Addicts may not know how to apply the information gathered at seminars - take the information learned and apply it to their individual beliefs or philosophies. These people suffer "loss of self" and have made seminars their "Higher Power."

Are you or someone you know addicted to SEMINARS?

Those who are may:

☐ Attend seminars constantly or become a groupie.

☐ Have an inability to apply information gathered in a personal way.

☐ Preach to others yet not practice what they preach.

☐ Spend unavailable money on seminars.

☐ Usually look for someone or something to fix them.

☐ Purchase books, tapes, etc. yet rarely read or listen to them.

☐ Argue with loved ones about seminars.

☐ Look to seminar leaders to give them an opinion.

☐ Put seminar leaders' thoughts and/or beliefs before their own.

☐ Attend a seminar in a crisis or to cure a crisis.

☐ Neglect other important personal needs to attend seminars.

☐ Become self-appointed promoters for seminars.

(Check page 9 for the Addiction Scale)

SERIOUSNESS ADDICTION

Seriousness Addicts are very depressing people to be around. They interpret most things as serious, even jokes. They view most things as larger than life. One theory is that they were emotionally terrorized as children and not protected from some of life's adult problems.

These problems were overwhelming for them to handle. Their caregivers probably did not explain minor problems to them as just being minor but reacted to them with panic, creating fear and a belief in the children that life is overwhelming and should be taken very seriously if they are to survive. Children internalize these feelings and beliefs, consequently carrying them into adulthood and the relationships they encounter.

Are you or someone you know addicted to SERIOUSNESS?

Those who are may:

- ☐ Feel out of control when things are not serious.
- ☐ Believe others take life too lightly.
- ☐ Look only for the negative in things to verify the seriousness.
- ☐ Frown most of the time.
- ☐ Have others who have grown impatient with their attitude.
- ☐ Be rigid in their negative beliefs, refusing to consider other possibilities.
- ☐ Have low self-esteem, seeing life as a threat vs. a journey.
- ☐ Live in constant fear of life, rarely seeking answers to the fear.
- ☐ Find that they become even more serious over the past few years.
- ☐ Attempt to convince others how serious life really is.
- ☐ Lose credibility with others due to their constant seriousness.
- ☐ Feel alone and frightened much of the time.

(Check page 9 for the Addiction Scale)

SEX ADDICTION

In this day and age, this particular addiction is much more dangerous and predominant than ever before. Sex Addicts may possess many of the same characteristics as Pornography Addicts, Prostitution Addicts and Voyeurism Addicts. Sex Addiction, however, is usually the primary addiction with all of the above. Sex Addicts are constantly haunted by the urge and compulsion to have sex and/or orgasm. One theory is that they deal with feelings via sex. They may avoid internal emotional pain by engaging in a sex act. Much like alcoholics, these people may be very credible in society, like clergy, counselors, doctors or corporate heads. The ratio between the sexes may very well be equal. This is an equal opportunity disease.

Are you or someone you know addicted to SEX?

Those who are may:

☐ Feel ashamed over sexual thoughts or behavior.

☐ Never feel totally satisfied or content from sex.

☐ Use sex to fix an argument or make up.

☐ Find that sex is the most important thing in their lives.

☐ Engage in sexual behavior that violates others.

☐ Masturbate several times a day.

☐ Feel a sense of power when engaging in sex.

☐ Experience uncontrollable sexual impulses.

☐ Generally view the opposite sex as sex objects.

☐ Have others express concern over their sexual preoccupation.

☐ Attempt to stop/control sexual behavior without success.

☐ Have problems in key areas of their lives
(work, school, etc.) due to sex.

(Check page 9 for the Addiction Scale)

SHAME ADDICTION

Unlike a chemical addiction, shame is a feeling. It is a feeling most try
to avoid. How then, do people become addicted to shame? One theory
is that they feel a tremendous amount of shame about their lives, so
much so that they feel unworthy as human beings. At this point, they
begin to discount, minimize or deny the good things that happen to
them. These people actually rely on the feeling of shame in an effort to
discount the positive things that happen to them, as well as to enforce
the belief that they're not worthy of positive things happening to them.
This becomes a vicious cycle that cannot be broken without outside
help. Others are very aware of the Shame addict's self-destructive
behavior and many times avoid these people in order to avoid the
negative messages they express.

Are you or someone you know addicted to SHAME?

Those who are may:

☐ Think they are basically bad people.

☐ Notice others avoiding them because they are so depressing.

☐ Feel defective and/or strange as human beings.

☐ Insist that they are unworthy people.

☐ Frequently do things to create negative attention.

☐ Feel like failures in life.

☐ Shame others around them on a regular basis.

☐ Increase shaming behavior over time.

☐ Avoid social situations because of shame.

☐ Feel relief after being shamed by themselves or others.

☐ Have loved ones who are constantly ashamed of them.

☐ Have an internal need to feel shame on a regular basis.

(Check page 9 for the Addiction Scale)

SHOPPING ADDICTION

Shopping Addicts are socially acceptable. People even make jokes about this addiction, which enables Shopping Addicts to continue their self-destructive behavior. The problem is that Shopping Addicts have a deep sense of remorse and low self-esteem. They get an emotional fix when shopping. Just like alcoholics use alcohol to medicate or avoid undesirable feelings, Shopping Addicts use shopping to accomplish the same thing. They are not confronting their pain or life issues directly. Shopping is a passive aggressive way of dealing with frustrations. Shopping Addicts, when angry, go shopping AT people. They keep their anger and frustration inside while expressing most feelings through shopping.

Are you or someone you know addicted to SHOPPING?

Those who are may:

☐ Shop regularly in order to relieve depression of unhappiness.

☐ "Shop till they drop" from exhaustion.

☐ Fear that they have a problem with shopping.

☐ Have frequent arguments with others about spending and shopping.

☐ Spend more money than they can afford.

☐ Frequently watch the shopping channels on television.

☐ Shop for unnecessary items at least twice weekly.

☐ Put off important tasks or commitments in order to go shopping.

☐ Frequently charge credit cards to their limit.

☐ Usually arrive early or before the stores are open.

☐ Notice others joke about them being a "shopaholic."

☐ Hide or sneak their purchases in order to avoid conflict.

(Check page 9 for the Addiction Scale)

SMILING ADDICTION

This addiction seems harmless on the surface; however, these people may be in great pain behind their smiles. They may never get a chance to express emotional pain because others have become dependent on them to project an image of happiness or being "OK." These people have learned to appear happy even while in crisis and almost to the point where it angers others. Others may have difficulty believing they are as happy or okay as they appear. The smile is phony and others know it. One theory is that when these people were children, they had to be the "peacekeepers" in the family. It was unsafe to express emotions in their families unless the emotion was good or positive according to their parents. These people learned to "look good" even at the cost of their self-esteem. They are afraid to express the truth about how they are truly feeling due to fear of rejection or abandonment by others. Their smile is a survival technique unconsciously used to cover-up their emotional pain.

Are you or someone you know addicted to SMILING?

Those who are may:

☐ Find that others suspect that their smile is not genuine.

☐ Smile when anger would seem more appropriate.

☐ Smile when hurt or sadness would seem more appropriate.

☐ Rarely express negative emotions directly to others.

☐ Make sure not to be seen without a smile.

☐ Be tired of smiling yet cannot seem to stop.

☐ Smile instead of crying.

☐ Feel like a phony, fearing others will find them out.

☐ Notice that others have difficulty connecting with them.

☐ Be the emotional caretaker for others.

☐ Rarely have an opinion on conflicting issues.

☐ Seem very rigid or controlled behind the smile.

(Check page 9 for the Addiction Scale)

SMOKING ADDICTION

This is the most deadly addiction in the United States, possibly in the world. Although it has become less popular, people continue to smoke and deny its consequences. Smoking separates people from each other at an emotional level. It is as though smokers use tobacco as a "smoke screen" while with others. Smoking is almost always a sign of damaged self-esteem. People become slaves to smoking and the rituals that go along with it. Smoking is one of the most difficult addictions from which to recover. Even those who are in other recovery programs (A.A., N.A., etc.) may continue to practice this addiction for years into their recovery. Many times, this addiction will be the killer of people who have successfully handled other very difficult addictions.

Are you or someone you know addicted to SMOKING?

Those who are may:

☐ Attempt to quit or cut back without success.

☐ Hear others express fear or concern over their smoking.

☐ Feel guilty or remorseful about smoking yet continue.

☐ Keep smokes around in case of an emergency.

☐ Panic when they run out of smokes.

☐ Smoke to calm their nerves.

☐ Continue to smoke even though it has caused physical problems.

☐ Increase intake of smokes since first beginning.

☐ Make promises to themselves and others to quit but can't.

☐ Smoke first thing in the morning.

☐ Hide, sneak or lie about smoking.

☐ Spend money on smokes before purchasing necessary items.

(Check page 9 for the Addiction Scale)

SNOOPING ADDICTION

America's most famous snoop was Mrs. Krabits from the old television series Bewitched. Snooping Addicts have nothing better to do than to snoop and gossip about others. They are generally bored and unhappy with their own lives. In an attempt to create some sort of distraction for the internal emotional conflict going on, these people will seek anyone or anything outside of themselves to focus on. They are generally disliked and rejected by others for this behavior, making life even more depressing. These people feel they are being helpful to others by watching out for them or the neighborhood. They are generally unaware of what a nuisance they are to others and fall victim to, "Why don't others appreciate me?" These people are angry a good portion of the time yet, rarely recognize it.

Are you or someone you know addicted to SNOOPING?

Those who are may:

☐ Make it a point to know everyone else's business.

☐ Often ask questions of or about others.

☐ Invade others' privacy on a regular basis.

☐ Often feel misunderstood by others.

☐ Have a sense of sneakiness about them.

☐ Seek thrills and adventure through snooping.

☐ Snoop to avoid depression or boredom.

☐ Have emotionally distant relationships with others.

☐ Search through others' belongings without permission.

☐ Watch neighbors and report to other disinterested parties.

☐ Have been in trouble several times for snooping yet continue to do it.

☐ Have an internal urge to snoop or can't stand not knowing.

(Check page 9 for the Addiction Scale)

SPENDING ADDICTION

A close relative to Shopping Addicts, Spending Addicts get a "rush" or release while in the act of spending money, as opposed to relief on completion of the act. Many times these people will make purchases, only to return the items soon afterward. This addiction is particularly damaging to marriage relationships. True Spending Addicts are out of control and, when confronted, they will go "underground" or become more secretive or sneaky about their addiction. The problem will continue to progress until these people self-destruct, destroy their relationships or receive help for this addiction. Department stores, television shopping channels and other vendors love these people. Those who seek intimacy with these people are in big trouble.

Are you or someone you know addicted to SPENDING?

Those who are may:

☐ Feel a "rush" when spending money.

☐ Lie about spending to avoid conflict, yet create conflict.

☐ Often experience shame or guilt over spending.

☐ Spend greater amounts of money and more frequently than before.

☐ Use credit cards irresponsibly for non-essential items.

☐ Be confronted by others about "abnormal" spending yet continue.

☐ Forget about money spent or what was purchased.

☐ Experience several financial problems from over-spending.

☐ Damage or destroy a relationship due to spending.

☐ Find that others are genuinely concerned over their spending.

☐ Attempt several methods at self-control, all ineffective.

☐ Spend to avoid or deny uncomfortable feelings.

(Check page 9 for the Addiction Scale)

SPORTS ADDICTION

An All American addiction, it separates families and friends fast. Sports Addicts many times become Gambling Addicts as well. The most dangerous part of this addiction is that Sports Addicts abandon their loved ones for sports. These people are obsessed with sports to the point that their lives revolve around it. For instance, the football addict is either watching football, thinking about football, playing football or betting on football. It would be very difficult to live with these people because, even when football is out of season, they are planning the next season. They are preoccupied with it to the point that it interferes with significant life issues and/or responsibilities.

Are you or someone you know addicted to SPORTS?

Those who are may:

☐ Participate in on-the-job gambling over sports.

☐ Have primary conversations around sports, while lacking intimacy.

☐ Neglect other responsibilities to participate in or watch sports.

☐ Use Sports to avoid intimacy with loved ones.

☐ Make sports the #1 priority in their lives while proceeding loved ones.

☐ Plan months in advance for their chosen sport's season.

☐ Argue with loved ones over time spent on sports.

☐ Expect others to have equal level of interest in sports.

☐ Religiously read the sports page of the newspaper.

☐ Keep detailed data on the players' stats, etc. in a particular sport.

☐ Spend more money than they can afford on sports.

☐ Rage when the sport/game is interrupted.

(Check page 9 for the Addiction Scale)

STEALING ADDICTION

Also known as "kleptomaniacs," Stealing Addicts generally feel intense anger or powerlessness. One theory about these people is that they had no healthy outlet to express feelings as children. They may have been repressed to the point that it wasn't safe to express feelings to others, particularly their parents. These people then may have become passive aggressive (acting out anger and repressed feelings in a covert or indirect manner) in an effort to release pent up frustration. The problem then is that these people eventually get caught and punished for not being direct about their feelings. In turn, this contributes to the feeling of powerlessness, making them act out the feelings in a deeper more hidden way. Stealing is one way these people ventilate the pent up frustration. This becomes a vicious cycle that they cannot control.

Are you or someone you know addicted to STEALING?

Those who are may:

☐ Feel a sense of power when stealing.

☐ Feel guilty when stealing yet do it anyway.

☐ Steal from family and friends.

☐ Experience a "high" or "rush" while stealing.

☐ Plan out stealing episodes in advance.

☐ Brag about stealing or what has been stolen.

☐ Have been arrested for stealing.

☐ Feel a sense of relief or accomplishment after stealing.

☐ Belong to a group or "ring" that steals or burglarizes.

☐ Steal more and more as time goes on.

☐ Put their lives in jeopardy because of stealing.

☐ Feel justified in stealing from others.

(Check page 9 for the Addiction Scale)

SUGAR ADDICTION

Sugar is a drug/food that has characteristics similar to speed or cocaine. Sugar brings people up or creates a quick feeling of euphoria followed by a crash or feeling down and tired. The mood swing is the same as in cocaine or amphetamine addictions but without the extreme euphoria. People become dependent on the "mini-high." Cravings are also present in the Sugar Addict. The #1 problem with this addiction is weight gain. The #2 problem is depression. Sugar is an additive in most junk food. This creates the craving for it. With the addictive cycle, these people become addicted to the sugar, gain weight, feel guilty and depressed and use the sugar to pull out of the depression, starting the vicious cycle all over again. Sugar is, for many, "Public Enemy #1."

Are you or someone you know addicted to SUGAR?

Those who are may:

☐ Frequently use sugar as a pick-me-up.

☐ Crave sugar at a particular time of day.

☐ Feel depressed, tired or angry a few hours after using sugar.

☐ Hear others comment or become concerned about their sugar intake.

☐ Experience undesirable weight gain due to excessive sugar intake.

☐ Have rotting or damaged teeth because of sugar.

☐ Sneak or hide candy or sugar.

☐ Use sugar several times a day.

☐ Suffer physical problems due to sugar consumption.

☐ Attempt to cut down on or stop sugar use without success.

☐ Develop a greater need for sugar to feel okay.

☐ Panic or become worried when sugar is not available.

(Check page 9 for the Addiction Scale)

TALKING ADDICTION

You will find these people constantly talking yet rarely saying anything significant or interesting. They are constantly "debriefing" (describing internal turmoil). The problem with Talking Addicts is that they never resolve the inner turmoil, nor do they realize they have any unresolved pain. One theory is that, when they were children these people witnessed others being abused and in turn, learned not to discuss the traumatic incident(s) overtly or directly with others, especially with the perpetrator and the victim. Talking Addicts may have repressed their pain over the years and now as adults, they talk constantly and pointlessly in an unconscious attempt to resolve the pain. Talking Addicts engage in repetitive and boring conversations.

Are you or someone you know addicted to TALKING?

Those who are may:

☐ Engage in repetitive/unresolved conversations with others.

☐ Feel that others attempt to avoid them and their conversations.

☐ Lose friends due to pointless conversations.

☐ Find that others have difficulty getting a word in while conversing with them.

☐ Be very boring to others and avoid intimacy.

☐ Lack boundaries (can't tell when others are bored/irritated).

☐ Rarely end a conversation; others have to do it.

☐ Constantly complain, yet never resolve their problems.

☐ Generally feel misunderstood by others.

☐ Suffer from loneliness due to others' avoidance.

☐ Have contemplated or attempted suicide due to this problem.

☐ Seek constant approval or validation from others.

(Check page 9 for the Addiction Scale)

TELEPHONE ADDICTION

This is a seemingly uncommon problem, yet my experience with one person suffering from this addiction is terrifying. Here, people attempting to express their concern or fear over this addiction are laughed at, not taken seriously or even shamed for having this addiction and not being able to control it. This addiction is no less destructive than any other. Society hides this problem very well, yet there are thousands who suffer from this problem and many who have taken their own lives as a result of it. Those suffering from this addiction have a tremendous need to talk about their pain. The shame they experience may be the reason they don't deal with others face-to-face. These people are in need of support and validation. Health will come about when they "come out of the closet" and discuss their pain openly, face-to-face with others.

Are you or someone you know addicted to the TELEPHONE?

Those who are may:

☐ Participate mostly in activities revolving around or taking place over the telephone.

☐ Become more isolated, fearing outside interference.

☐ Spend hours on the phone, often with unknown people.

☐ Have an astronomically high and unaffordable phone bill.

☐ Feel depressed and guilty over constant telephone activity.

☐ Avoid other chores and responsibilities to be on the telephone.

☐ Contemplate suicide over telephone addiction.

☐ Be forced to make payment arrangements with the phone company.

☐ Feel panic or at a loss if not close to the phone.

☐ Steal money to pay phone bills in order to avoid disconnection.

☐ Abandon most social activities to be on the phone.

☐ Have decreased self-esteem due to preoccupation with the telephone.

(Check page 9 for the Addiction Scale)

TELEVISION ADDICTION

Television is our all-American pastime. Some people lose their entire identity in this electronic babysitter. Television is obviously mood altering. It can take people who are feeling depressed and, in 15 minutes, have them smiling. The danger to all this is that these people become dependent on the television to feel!! It becomes a tool to avoid conversation, negative feelings and, most of all, intimacy. Most people need intimate, emotional contact with others. Television separates us from our needs. Many problems are encountered as a result of this addiction - physical problems, emotional problems, sexual problems, the list goes on. Once people become addicted to the television, it is difficult to elicit their participation in real life.

Are you or someone you know addicted to TELEVISION?

Those who are may:

☐ Watch television during most free time.

☐ Rely on television as their soul source of information.

☐ Frequently fall asleep while watching television.

☐ Be preoccupied with television and be able to identify most programs.

☐ Find that their anxiety gets greater as they get more involved in television.

☐ Have frequent arguments over watching too much television.

☐ Feel panic or worry if they can't watch television.

☐ Neglect exercise and become a "couch potato."

☐ Neglect responsibilities by watching television.

☐ Damage intimacy in a relationship by watching television.

☐ Abandon most social activities to watch television.

☐ Know or fear a problem exists because of television.

(Check page 9 for the Addiction Scale)

TERROR ADDICTION

This is an addiction in which people have a need to terrorize or frighten themselves or others. These people may need terror just to feel!! Everyday feelings are not stimulating enough. Halloween is their favorite holiday. Scary movies, haunted houses and practical jokes that are frightening to others are the typical activities of Terror Addicts. Others usually think there is something wrong with these people. Terror Addicts (much like Danger Addicts) may be out of touch with their feelings (emotionally) and, in turn, resort to physical risk just to experience feelings. These people are seldom nurturing to others in a relationship. They are unpredictable, emotionally unbalanced and insensitive to others' fears or feelings. When you meet a Terror Addict, unless you are one yourself, turn around and run the other direction.

Are you or someone you know addicted to TERROR?

Those who are may:

☐ Routinely frighten others.

☐ Put others' safety in jeopardy by their terrorist behavior.

☐ Have an inability to sense the fears and needs of others (lack boundaries).

☐ Have had accidents due to the frightening behavior.

☐ Be preoccupied (thinking about or planning) with frightening things.

☐ Have prior arrests due to frightening behavior.

☐ Have an internalized drive (urge) to experience terror.

☐ Lose friends or loved ones because of terrorizing behavior.

☐ Lack remorse for others' misfortunes.

☐ Need to frequent thrill rides (roller coasters, etc.).

☐ Have an increased need to experience greater and greater terror.

☐ Deny or minimize the problem when confronted by others.

(Check page 9 for the Addiction Scale)

THERAPY ADDICTION

Therapy Addicts are usually looking for a "Higher Power" or someone to take responsibility for their lives. They become dependent on their therapists to "fix" them. They lose sight of the fact that they are responsible for making decisions and for handling the consequences of those decisions. Therapy Addicts have a tremendous need to be heard or validated by others. The man off the street isn't good enough to validate them; they prefer to blame a professional. These people appear to be making an effort at change; however in reality they are hiding out in therapy as a way of avoiding change. Therapy Addicts fear life. It is common for these people to "therapize" or preach to others about the value of therapy, yet lack credibility with others due to their own lack of change.

Are you or someone you know addicted to THERAPY?

Those who are may:

☐ Be in therapy for years without significant change.

☐ Rely 90% on the therapist's opinion or have none.

☐ Develop resentment toward the therapist.

☐ Feel totally lost without therapy.

☐ Spend most of their money on therapy, usually resenting it.

☐ Conduct diagnostic interviews with unwilling friends.

☐ Have relationships that have suffered while they were preoccupied with therapy.

☐ Be seen by others as a "therapy junkie."

☐ Use "psycho-babble" when relating to others.

☐ Need a therapy "fix" in order to get through the week.

☐ Avoid intimacy for years by staying in therapy.

☐ Have difficulty feeling without being in a therapist's office.

(Check page 9 for the Addiction Scale)

VICTIMIZATION ADDICTION

The comic strip Ziggy is a prime example of this addiction. No matter what, these people seem to attract self-defeating situations. That is the basis of this addiction.

One theory is that these people have never felt worthy of success or good things happening to them. Others may want to avoid these people because of bad luck. Murphy's Law seems to have been invented by them. Always looking for validation as victims, these people will go to any lengths to attract others' attention to their misfortunes.

Are you or someone you know addicted to VICTIMIZATION?

Those who are may:

☐ Constantly experience self-pity.

☐ Feel their bad luck has become greater and more consistent over time.

☐ Attempt to convince others of the tragedy of it all.

☐ Lose control over daily living due to this problem.

☐ Generally think about or experience bad luck.

☐ Be observed by others to enjoy this problem.

☐ Make regular unsuccessful attempts to change.

☐ Feel like, "I never get a break."

☐ Often have thoughts of suicide or depression.

☐ Blame others for their misfortunes.

☐ Generally be self-centered.

☐ Have others give up on them ever changing.

(Check page 9 for the Addiction Scale)

VOYEURISM ADDICTION

A voyeur is a Peeping Tom type. These people invade others' privacy, usually without them ever knowing it. Voyeurism Addicts have low self-esteem. This problem is different from exhibitionism. These people feel powerless, yet, when peeping, they feel powerful in that their victims have no control because they usually don't know they are victims. Voyeurs are usually harmless to others in the physical sense but extremely self-destructive in the psychological sense. As with any addiction, voyeurs have an insatiable need to continue the behavior in order to relieve a sense of guilt from the previous episode of peeping.

Are you or someone you know addicted to VOYEURISM?

Those who are may:

☐ Secretly watch others without their knowledge.

☐ Have a perverted sense of sexuality.

☐ Fear sex, yet fantasize about it.

☐ Have previously been confronted or arrested for their behavior.

☐ Spend hours watching or planning to watch someone.

☐ Often experience guilt or shame over voyeurism.

☐ Purchase binoculars or a telescope for voyeurism.

☐ Have intense body feelings when secretly watching others.

☐ Watch others to relieve loneliness or depression.

☐ Prefer voyeurism to being in a relationship.

☐ Damage their self-esteem due to voyeurism.

☐ Experience a sense of power when watching others.

(Check page 9 for the Addiction Scale)

WORK ADDICTION

Commonly referred to as workaholics, these people not only deny their behavior but also have it reinforced by most people. In most situations, a hard worker is a positive thing. However, when it comes to Work Addiction, these people are not only self-destructive but destructive to the organization as well. They may become resentful for not being validated by the boss or appreciated by the family for their hard work, even though they have abandoned their families for work. Work Addicts expect rewards but would never admit to it. They are dependent upon others to validate their worth as people. They become "human doings" and forget they are human beings. They are so wrapped up in the work that they lose sight of other important aspects of their lives.

Are you or someone you know addicted to WORK?

Those who are may:

☐ Emotionally or physically abandon others for work.

☐ Lose sleep or rest over work.

☐ Regularly work through lunch.

☐ Experience difficulty relaxing.

☐ Work to avoid conflict or intimacy.

☐ Work to avoid undesirable feelings.

☐ Become resentful when accomplishments are not recognized.

☐ Forget important tasks or commitments not related to work.

☐ Constantly think about or talk about work.

☐ Feel that enough is never enough.

☐ Be overly critical of others' work.

☐ Feel out of control and powerless over having to work.

(Check page 9 for the Addiction Scale)

WORRY ADDICTION

These people have a need to worry. Worrying takes the focus off the real problem (which is usually unresolved emotional pain dating back many years). Being around Worry Addicts is difficult for others because they are constantly making negative comments, being pessimistic and believing the worst has or is about to happen. Worry Addicts rarely understand what others are telling them. They live in their own little world of fantasy, and even when they seem to be listening to positive comments from others, they are secretly thinking, "This person is just saying this to make me feel better; the good stuff will never happen." Worrying is a survival role for Worry Addicts. Anyone attempting to stop the worry will be frustrated at the constant failure of his or her attempts.

Are you or someone you know addicted to WORRY?

Those who are may:

☐ Insist on the negative aspect of most situations.

☐ Regularly lose sleep or rest due to worrying.

☐ Constantly worry about others' issues.

☐ Lack a sense of most feelings other than fear.

☐ Expect the worst or that something will go wrong.

☐ Worry without evidence of a potential problem.

☐ Drink or use drugs to reduce worry and anxiety.

☐ Lose control of important aspects of their lives due to worrying.

☐ Be resented or avoided by others who want to avoid their negativity.

☐ Experience medical problems due to worrying.

☐ Worry more and more over minor issues as time goes by.

☐ Feel powerless over worrying, so why change?

(Check page 9 for the Addiction Scale)

About the Author

Tim Chapman, Msc.D, CSAC

Tim Chapman is an internationally recognized addiction counselor. His three decades of experience include living, learning, teaching about and treating the problem of addiction.

Tim is a professional trainer, counselor and corporate consultant on addiction. He is well known from California to Honk Kong. His studies and credentials include A Masters and Doctorate degree in Metaphysics, Certified Alcoholism Counselor, University of California at Irvine, Certified Alcohol and Drug Abuse Counselor, California Association of Alcohol and Drug Abuse Counselors, Level II Certified Clinical Supervisor, National

Certification Board of Alcohol and Drug Abuse Counselors. Tim's enthusiasm is contagious! He is a sought after speaker due to his extensive experience on radio and television throughout his career. He has authored another book, *Midolescence: Handling the Twenty-Six-Year-Old Teenager*, available in paperback on Amazon.com, and is a columnist for the *Orange County Register*, a Pulitzer Prize winning newspaper.

Tim has designed six hospital based treatment programs for addiction as well as numerous outpatient clinics here and abroad.

Presently, Tim is the Executive Director of Teensavers™ a unique program for adolescents suffering from substance abuse, emotional and behavioral problems. Tim created the "6-Basic Feelings" theory which is utilized in his adult and adolescent residential treatment programs.

To reach Tim log onto www.teensavers.com, email him at tim@teensavers.com, or call 1-800-451-1947.